Running Into the

Petri Dish of

BURNOUT

A How Not-To Guide

Running Into the

Petri Dish of

BURNOUT

A How Not-To Guide

Laurie McGinley

Book Cover by Rich Rizzo

First edition 2025

ISBN: 979-8-9927329-0-0

Acknowledgments

Thank you to the love of my life, Amelia, who has helped me be more me for over two decades and has endured more BS from me as I've transformed and healed than anyone deserves in a lifetime.

To the littles, it is you who inspire me, every day, to find new ways to do better and be more present.

Thank you to my coaches and teachers– especially David, Kate, and Sharleen – who have pushed me, lovingly, towards discomfort and growth.

Thank you to MJ, who carried this book to term while maintaining my truth, my voice, and my story. I could not have done this without you.

Table of Contents

Read this intro.

Hey you.

Yeah, you.

You don't have time to waste.

That's why—and this might sound counterintuitive—I want you to *slow down*.

I'd like you to read the intro, even if you skim the rest of the book. I knooooow, it's the 21st century, and we're all doing what we can with goldfish-quality attention spans, but please hear me out for the next 12 pages.

I want to tell you about how I face-planted into the Petri Dish of Burnout when I was only 31.

I had ascended into my dream role at a great architecture firm. I was young, high-achieving, and on my way up. Sure, I was spending my evenings and weekends working. Sure, I was firing on all cylinders in every area of my life. Sure, my efforts to revolutionize the industry were feeling futile and existential. But this was what I always wanted. *Right?*

Well, then, I had a frickin' *stroke*.

At the time, the stroke caught me completely by surprise, but looking back, it's obvious to me that having a stroke was a completely predictable consequence of how burned out I was. I understand now that I not only *let* burnout happen, I *manifested* that burnout. I conjured it. I brewed up a giant potion of burnout, *without realizing that I was following a very predictable recipe.*

Friend: I wrote this book because if you haven't burned out yet, <u>I don't want the same thing to happen to you</u>. And if you have already burnt out, I don't want your experience to have been for nothing.

I burned out because I cared a lot: about my work, about my values, about the planet, about being good and doing good. In the 16 years between my stroke and writing this book, I've made it my goal to help passionate people like me. I created a business in which I serve as a speaker and guide, helping them to harness their energy like a hyper-sensitive and powerful solar panel and do *awesome* things with it, instead of accidentally using it to turbocharge their collision into the pavement when they faceplant. Others in my line of work use the word "coach," but I prefer "guide" for reasons I'll get into later.

In my work, I get to meet and support a lot of other people who *also* care a lot. Some of them burned out before I met them. Some of them burned out right before my eyes. Others were at risk of burning out, but made smart choices and escaped that fate.

Over the years, I've realized that those of us who lead with love and who care about doing good in the world are susceptible to a unique type of burnout, different from the kind that afflicts get-rich-quick schemers or that haunts corporate drones. It's a kind of burnout that I haven't seen written or talked about directly.

Our strain of burnout is deeper and more existential, a world-weariness that can only come from committing one's life to addressing global challenges (like championing climate solutions) that deserve and require our focused minds and whole hearts.

We don't have time to *not* address that type of burnout. The people who experience it are too important to this world. That's why I can't waste my time or talent, and why I'm sharing everything I know about this theme. I'm *super* not in the mood for climate change to interrupt my plans to watch my children grow up, and I'm assuming you have your own plans that don't involve continuously being displaced by climate-related catastrophes.

You can't waste time, either. We can't afford for you to run around in circles, wasting your unique talents. If you're part of a team that isn't meshing or reaching its potential— and especially if you are the one *leading* that team—you have a responsibility to help break that cycle. Leaders who burn themselves out do worse than waste their own time and talent—they waste the time and talent of *everyone on their team*, too.

People with bright ideas, benevolent values, and high ambition have the ability to change the world. Heck, I'll say it: they're the only people with the ability to *save* the world. (Yes, this world, the one that's spinning wildly out of control under the force of the climate crisis, insurmountable international conflict, systemic oppression, and our collective inability to respond to any of them.)

The thing that's so nefarious about this strain of burnout is that it's caused by an abundance of love, a spilling-over of conviction, and the dysphoria of pushing forward an initiative that societal inertia is trying to reject.

In other words, the qualities that make people capable of leading the world into a brighter future are unfortunately the very same qualities that inevitably lead them directly into what I call "the Petri Dish of Burnout."

This book is *not* a comprehensive manual on overcoming burnout, and it's not trying to be that. Lord knows, there's no shortage of books and resources out there that fit that description. Let me save you some time and tell you the two key ways that this book is *distinct* from others, so that you can know if and how to use it:

1. It's focused specifically on people who are working in climate (and other values-based sectors) and the unique challenges they face.

2. Instead of making generalizations about why burnout is similar for everyone, we'll look at why burnout is *different* for everyone who experiences it, including the burnout "styles" of four common personality types among people who lead initiatives in climate.

Who this book is for

Read closely, dear reader. This section is especially important.

The too long; didn't read (tl;dr) is that this book is, broadly, *for* and *about* **ambitious leaders**, especially **people who are working on climate initiatives.** But it will be useful to anyone who is a member of a team with these key qualities:

- Your team is trying to do something important and positive in the world. It might be guiding climate direction at a corporation, a campaign or office of an elected official, a one-person team, a non-profit organization, or even an intentional community. What matters is that your team is (at least theoretically) driven by a mission and a set of values.

- Your team is being led in a way that is either putting the team at risk of burnout, or that is already past the point of burnout. Your team should be open to changing things—even if the members of the team don't agree on what those changes need to be.

- Your team is led by a person who, on good days, we'd call motivated and ambitious and, on bad days, we'd call mercurial and harsh. These qualities are both what makes them such a great leader, and also what makes them likely to overwork themselves and/or their team.

- You are personally motivated to support the success of the initiative you are working on.

This book is also for you if you're willing to indulge my ulterior motive here: that you *pass this book around to people who need it.* There are a few "types" of people who I hope will find it helpful, and this book will be at its most useful when people help each other to access the tricks I've learned for overcoming burnout.

The first "type" is the broadest, but also the most important: I'm talking about **leaders**. By that I mean C-suite employees, founders, and directors—as well as the folks who are forging ahead courageously in *supporting* roles within climate-oriented initiatives. Leadership is relative. You are leaders, too, even if your role, current responsibilities, and paycheck don't reflect that fact. In any event, this book will give you food for thought about how you carry yourself as a leader, and how to work well with other leaders, including the person you report to.

The other "types" are more nuanced and subjective. By identifying these four types, I'm attempting to help you recognize yourself and the people you work with—and the ways in which burnout (and its opposite) can play a role in your journey. I'll introduce them quickly now so that, if you want, you can skip right to the part about your "type," where I'll go into much more detail.

These types are **Perfectionists, Heroes, Researchers**, and **Motivators**. There are lots of ways I can describe them, but the quickest way for you to self-identify is <u>the thing that you feel is slowing you down.</u>

For **Perfectionists,** it's a sense that you have too many tabs open on your browser and tasks you need to button up — often combined with a lack of sleep. For **Heroes**, it's frustration that you can't do everything you want to, but you are resistant to scaling down. For **Researchers**, it's feeling that no one on your team understands you or your vision. For **Motivators**, it's impatience with people who can't keep up.

It's possible you may not recognize yourself among these four personality types. You can still derive insights from this book, even if your type is not represented among these characters, because you will encounter these formidable personalities, especially in the climate sector.

(If these types sound familiar, it is because they overlap with four of the nine Enneagram personality types. Perfectionists are Ones; Heroes are Threes; Researchers are Fives; and Motivators are Eights. I renamed these types to make this book accessible to readers who are not familiar with the Enneagram types.)

What's in this book?

Let me level with you: I don't read a lot of books. I'm more distractible than a—hey, did you see that puppy?

I'm not writing this book for my own gratification. I'm writing it because I learned some really important lessons as a result of doing things like destroying my body, torpedoing my career, and spoiling my own talent for a really long time.

In short, I landed inside an oozy, disgusting, pulsating blob that is constantly growing in a place I call the Petri Dish of Burnout. I'll tell you all about it later, but for now all you need to know is that the world needs your talents too much for me to let you get stuck in there, too.

The theme of this book is burnout, but it's also about the *opposite* of burnout (which I'll reveal to you on page 159.) It's about leadership, conviction, fear, love, mindfulness, growth, and running. (Most of the stuff about running is metaphorical, so don't put on your shoes just yet.)

In this book, I discuss these themes in three main ways:

1. Telling you about how I came to understand the patterns in my own life that led *me* into the Petri Dish of Burnout.

2. Illustrating how the people I've worked with were susceptible to burnout *because* of their greatest strengths.

3. Sharing some lessons, recommendations, and exercises that will help you to avoid or escape the Petri Dish of Burnout yourself.

How to use this book

I suggest reading it, but it's probably handy as a flyswatter (unless you're reading the e-version; I don't recommend killing mosquitoes with a tablet).

But seriously folks…

- You can read it cover to cover. There's a logical progression to it, so the things I say make a bit more sense if you read it sequentially.

- You can skim it. No really, I won't be offended. In fact, I <u>so</u> won't be offended that I even wrote a summary to go at the start of each chapter. I'm not exactly Stephen King over here, there's no suspense to be found. Consider yourself spoiler-alerted or whatever the kids are saying these days.

- You can look at the table of contents and pick the chapters or sections that are calling out to you.

  o A side note: If you plan to skip ahead to one of the lessons about the four personality types (4 for Perfectionists, 5 for Heroes, 6 for Researchers, 7 for Motivators), I strongly recommend you read the intro to section 2 (on page 67) *beforehand*. And then I recommend you fast forward to the parting advice directed to your personality type in lesson 9.

- But most of all, I hope you consider sharing this book with the other people on your team and in your community. One of my primary arguments is that the work of resisting burnout occurs much more quickly and deeply when you approach it as a group and with support. (See? Full of spoilers.)

Whatever you do, though, do _not_ mistake reading a book with undergoing change. In the same way that reading a cookbook does not make you Samin Nosrat and watching the Olympics does not make you Simone Biles, reading this book is not the same as doing meaningful work. It can't be. At best, it will be the spark that gets you started.

My ulterior motive, which I'll lay on the table for you, is that the hugely important people who are team members on those initiatives read this book first. And then, when enough of them recommend it to their supervisors, employers, and mentors, they'll read it, too. They're gonna need help because most of them won't listen until they've alienated too many people, things get dire, or enough of you tell them to pay attention.

A note about the characters

In the second section of this book, I'll introduce you to four people: Olive, Trip, Fiona, and Eisen. They represent a cross-section of my clients, but they are _not_ real people. Think of them as amalgamations of each of the four personality types (Perfectionists, Heroes, Researchers, and Motivators, respectively). In other words, they're true stories in the form of fiction, presented in a way that illustrates the themes of the book in a concise and accessible way. This also protects the privacy of my clients.

(For my Enneagram fans: I left you an Easter egg when I named these characters. Their names start with the same letter that their Enneagram personality type begins with:

Olive is a One; Trip is a Three; Fiona is a Five; and Eisen is an Eight. I know, I know, it's unbearably clever.)

Let's go, already!

I know. You're impatient. So am I. That's something that makes us awesome.

Many of us, when we care really deeply about what we do (or what we aspire to be doing), cannot reconcile the importance of our work with the limits of our minds, bodies, souls, resources, and relationships. So we do something really stupid: we jeopardize the work. We overthink our choices, overexert ourselves and our team, or fail to navigate the emotional aspects of the work.

When work is meaningful, we need to create a sense of balance. This looks different for everyone. For some of us, that involves learning to reflect before we act. For others, it's learning to be more trusting and improvisational. Still others are learning to manage anxiety and resist its pull. As I'll discuss: you *can* accomplish these things on your own. It just takes forever, and, as I said at the very beginning of this intro, *we don't have time for you to take the scenic route.* Your team needs to achieve balance, resist burnout, and contribute its amazing gifts—as soon as possible.

I have good news and bad news:

The bad news is that this is hard, soul-searching work.

The good news is that there are ways to get there 10x faster, and **I'm about to show them to you.**

Section 1

Stretch Your Hammies.

Lesson 1

Running balls-out* feels amazing, but you won't get anywhere.

(*it's not what you think)

SUMMARY: "Running balls-out" is a metaphor for making the same mistake repeatedly for the sake of a perceived expectation, instead of learning your lesson and forming a new pattern in your behavior. Great example: I gave up cross country running in order to focus on architecture, but in both places I continued a habit of pushing myself and others to their limits, which royally backfired. If "burnout" is a destination, then running "balls-out" is a way to get there while convincing yourself otherwise. Your capital-A Awesome is a strength, but it's also a potential weakness when you harness its power to run balls-out.

Okay, I'd better tell you what the heck balls-out means, so you can rest assured that this book does not describe an exhibitionist method of jogging.

It's about to get really nerdy, but don't worry, there won't be a quiz.

There's a mechanical instrument called a centrifugal governor, which is a part of many steam engines. It's a short metal axis near the engine's release valve. You can recognize it by its pair of spinning, steel balls. It looks like this:

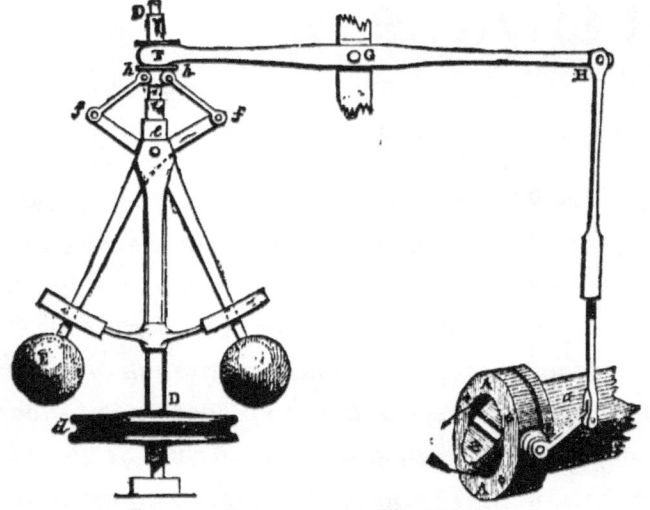

FIG. 4.---*Governor and Throttle-Valve.*   1

When pressure and heat build within the engine, it propels the centrifugal governor's spinning motion, balls and all. The higher the pressure, the faster the centrifugal

---

1 https://en.wikipedia.org/wiki/Centrifugal_governor

governor spins, and the higher the balls go. When the spinning force is strong enough, the balls stretch out horizontally away from the axis, which we colloquially call "running balls-out." When this happens, the balls trigger a mechanism that tells the engine to cool down now.

In short, the centrifugal governor is a safety mechanism. When it's going balls-out, it's saying "You've gotta calm down, bruh," though not literally. "Keep shoveling that coal, but don't melt me."

Okay, you might be saying, why do we need a synonym for burnout that sounds X-rated? And that would be a fair question.

Running balls-out is closely *connected* to burnout, but it's not the same thing. Think of it this way: they're different parts of speech.

Burnout is the crash. Burnout is rock bottom. Burnout is a destination. Burnout is the Petri Dish I'll be telling you about later.

So, if burnout is a destination, then running balls-out is a journey. But it's not even a profound journey or anything, it's more like a hamster wheel. Running balls-out is keeping going despite (or because of) copious warning signals. Running balls-out is scrambling away from rock bottom. Running balls-out is twiddling your thumbs in purgatory while you put off your inevitable escalator ride down. Running balls-out is screaming, quietly, behind your eyes, because you're stuck doing work that feels mediocre while knowing that you're capable of achieving *so much more.*

"But Laurie," you might be saying, "I *need* to run balls-out. I have to pay my staff. I have to feed my family. Everyone is counting on me. If we don't close this funding round the company will be doomed." Or, "If I don't get this product to market, the coral will be lost forever." Or, "If I don't implement this technology, millions of farmers will be taken advantage of. I don't have time to slow down."

And to that I say: you actually don't have time *not* to slow down.

World changers think they've outsmarted their bodily limits by pushing themselves within a hair's breadth of needing to slow down. They keep themselves riiiiiight at the edge of the cliff, and applaud themselves for not falling off. In this reality, though, they feel satisfied at having created and stuck to their own limits, but are unaware that doing so actually stalls them more than intentionally slowing down does.

Running balls-out is something people did when steam locomotives were the future and, in case you haven't noticed, we've upgraded to faster methods.

Imagine you're the person shoveling the coal into the steam engine. You're kicking ass at this, doing your hardest work at a version of your job that's been determined by a railroad baron. You're giving your work your stinking all to hit an imaginary target that you *choose* to limit your sights on.

Running balls-out is hamster-wheeling it while thinking you are Sha'Carri Richardson.

And for us and our efforts to repair our broken world, we can't spend all our energy running balls-out. When we're distracted and ineffective, we give corrupt and rapacious institutions the perfect opening to jump in and infect the world with more of their greedy goo. All the while, we're convinced that if we just run faster, push harder, get through one more week like this, everything will change!

It won't change. Not like that.

You might think you're going as fast as you can because you're *used to the feeling of running balls-out*. It's what's gotten you to the podium over and over again in your life, so of course you're attached to it, and you believe it's the best way forward from here. But it isn't.

Now, before you think I'm coming at you saying I was born with the self-restraint to do this automatically, let me reassure you that I've run balls-out a time or two in my life (and I still do, occasionally). I understand the impulse. I've seen the Petri Dish of Burnout, people—and it's not pretty.

But my journey into the Petri Dish begins the way all journeys into the Petri Dish do: with the discovery of a particular kind of Awesome.

Running in ropes

I was practicing with my high school cross country team when I first noticed that my heart was bigger than the chest cavity in which it resides.

I grew up in a small, rural town called Mauston, Wisconsin and in the early 90s went to a high school with about 500 students total. We all dreaded the days when coach DeVoe would have us "run in ropes." Running in ropes felt like a draconian method of torture, but it was really just a way to build team camaraderie and to encourage us to intentionally pace ourselves. Groups of up to nine of us would be "leashed" around our waists, all of us tethered to one center loop of rope.

It's easy to understand why everyone hated running-in-ropes days. The fastest kids hate it because they spend a lot of time pulling their slower peers and feeling frustrated. The slowest kids hate it because they spend a lot of time being dragged by their faster peers and feeling humiliated.

Hooray! Equal opportunity torture!

But don't worry, we ran in a perfectly safe environment: the gravel shoulder of a highway with a 55 mph speed limit. Uphill, both ways.

The day I realized how awesome I was coincided with a workout that was particularly difficult, even for this setup, because we'd just had a big race a few days before. Everyone was *really* tired. I remember specifically that my quads were burning.

One of the rules of running in ropes is that everyone takes turns leading. When it was my turn, I maneuvered myself to the front of the pack and tried to pick up the pace. The rope's chokehold around my waist tightened, and my teammates grunted in disapproval. It was uncomfortable for all of us.

Through heavy breathing, I wheezed, "I know you're tired! I'm tired, too! Let's work together and get this hill behind us."

And then I felt the most amazing thing: the rope around my waist relaxed. The eight other runners were matching my pace. Their faces relaxed. They eased into the gait. They encouraged each other. All because I'd encouraged *them*.

This happened during a period of my life when I was feeling isolated, overwhelmed, and unsafe in just about every possible way. This moment was a glimpse of how unlimited our potential was, and how effortlessly we were able to access more of it.

My heart expanded, enveloping my eight peers into it.

It was intoxicating. I'd never done anything like that before. As we crested the hill united in a sense of accomplishment, suddenly I needed to know: was that a fluke? Or had my heart always been big enough to hold eight people in it? And if so, could it hold more?

I began experimenting.

Homecoming

The biggest event of the year in Mauston was the homecoming football game. It's not every day that the middle school marching band combines forces with the high school marching band for the halftime show. (Eat your heart out, Janet Jackson!)

I played the quads. You've seen them: the set of four drums that usually lead the cadence and get a few fancy solos. The decades of back pain I've endured since carrying the quads for four years was totally worth it. I played the heck out of those drums. And I took it *very* seriously.

So imagine my horror when my bandmates chose the moment we were lining up to march to start goofing off. Chatting with each other. Picking their nails. Playing stupid clapping games. Everything other than focusing.

The middle and high school band teachers were no match for 200 teenagers.

So I started the cadence on the quads, loud enough to startle all my peers and get them to shut up. It took just a couple seconds for my impromptu drum solo to capture everyone's attention. I paused for a moment to bring them all into my heart, and then I shouted to them. Something like, "It's time to get into show mode, everyone! This is what we've been waiting and practicing for! So let's focus and get ready for our moment!"

This was probably pretty humbling for my band teacher, Mr. Spindler, who simply nodded his head in thanks, and took over.

All at once, 200 teenage musicians turned their attention to Mr. Spindler. With the attention off of me, I felt like I was radiating light and heat. I had brought *200 people* into my heart.

Now, my peers probably thought of me as an annoying goody-goody tattle-tale type. I had never totally fit in, and I doubt if anyone else matched my excitement about our marching band tooting and banging away in a relatively small clearing among acres and acres of cornfields. For goodness' sake, there was a tractor parked within view of the game.

But I didn't care. The show we put on felt absolutely legendary to me.

Was it possible?, I wondered, *Can it get even bigger than this?*

I had found a superpower that felt amazing. A way that I could lead people, inspire people, activate people.

I felt like I could do anything I wanted with that power.

I now have the language to say that my passion for motivating people was, and still is, my Awesome.

You and <u>your</u> awesome

How about you? When did *you* first realize what *your* Awesome is?

Okay, I realize that sounds like a sleazy pickup line, but I want you to really sit with that question for a moment. Because knowing what your Awesome is is more than a self-congratulatory ritual. It's a diagnostic tool.

Your Awesome is the skill you have that can be used to repair and transform the world. It's the superpower you announce, by name, in the opening credits of the Captain

America cartoon. Understanding what your Awesome is and where it comes from is essential to knowing how to use it.

In addition to savoring the awesomeness of your Awesome, identifying your Awesome is also the first step in recognizing how it *also* makes you vulnerable to burnout.

So one more time:

When did *you* first realize what *your* Awesome is?

Running through the pain

Fast-forward a few years. I left Wisconsin for Minneapolis, where I could run and study Architecture. I was a Division 1 student athlete at the University of Minnesota, where I went *all-in* on cross country.

Our coach assigned us a nine-day running program to keep us in shape during the winter break between semesters, which I diligently followed (of course). On day two, I started to notice some foot discomfort, but I forged ahead, and ran a total of 75 miles. Even though I knew that something was wrong. Even though I was aware enough to ice my foot.

On the ninth and final day of that program, I ran 15 miles. It took two hours. Every single step was excruciating, but at least the record would show: I executed the program.

On the tenth day, the training office was open. I went in there at 8am and I left in a walking cast.

This is how running balls-out works: You execute the program. Somebody (perhaps yourself) tells you how to succeed, and you do it because you want to affirm that you're stronger than everybody else around you. In a way, this came from the same impulse that led me to push my peers to be focused during the halftime show in high school, except I was only pushing *myself*.

People like you and me, we don't *quit*. That would be admitting defeat. And I couldn't do that. So I kept running.

One day, as I was leaving the pool in the University of Minnesota fitness center, I bumped into the school's resident sports psychologist.

"I see you working out a lot," she said, underlining that phrase: *a lot*.

I was an extremely stubborn 19-year-old, and so I thought I heard awe in her voice. I told her about my schedule: stationary bike six days a week and the pool one day a week, cross training with other injured athletes.

"That's a lot to manage," she said, "not to mention a full course load. And I heard you're an Honors student?"

"In all my classes," I replied.

"How's your foot healing?"

"It's getting there," I told her.

It wasn't.

"How are you managing all of that?"

I assured her it was all under control. I scheduled my days in 15-minute increments from 6:00 a.m. to 10:00 p.m. and, needless to say, I wasn't setting aside time to have fun. The chaos of a freshman dorm was happening all around me—the people on my floor were getting drunk for the first time, making out and doing other nonsense—but I just shut the door, so me and my bachelors-and-masters-in-five-years roommate could study all night.

Her eyebrows shot straight up, and I realized that she wasn't impressed, she was worried.

"Any chance I can snag a time slot in your busy schedule sometime soon?"

"Sure," I told her. "I can fit you in tomorrow at 7:00 a.m., but then don't have a free slot until next week."

"... 7:00 a.m.it is, then."

In retrospect, I was probably a terrifying student to deal with.

We can get so attached to stories of who we are that we'll fight like hell to keep those stories true. We'll pretty much bludgeon other people with our insistence—but that's nothing compared to the violence we do to ourselves.

Until that chance encounter with the sports psychologist, I had been destroying my body in my attempt to prove I wasn't injured. Under the surface, I was poisoning myself with denial. My enormous, beautiful heart was being neglected in favor of a familiar story that felt safe: I was a high-achieving cross country runner.

So when I talked to the sports psychologist, my soul left my body and I went into autopilot. I don't remember a single blessed word from the conversation, I just remember being confronted with the crushing truth: I could not continue with my insane attempts to ignore my injury. I needed to make dramatic changes in my life. It felt like the molecular bonds holding my body together would slacken and give up, like my life force would leak out of me and form a useless puddle right there on her office floor. I could not accept what she was telling me, and yet I could not walk away and act like it wasn't true.

The "me" who arrived in that conversation was not the "me" who departed from it.

I made the choice to quit, but I hadn't accepted it enough to tell anyone or do anything about it.

A week went by.

Then two.

When the pain in my right foot was too acutely painful, I decided to use my left foot while driving. The pain rang out like a bell, telling me "It's over, dude." Around and around the track I went.

A third week.

A fourth.

I occasionally used my bike to get around, even though I was on crutches. I tried to convince myself it was fine if I just modified the way I rode and put my heel on the pedal. But it became more and more inevitable and obvious that the choice had been made for me. For Pete's sake, after I parked my bike, I'd untie my *walking cane* from the crossbar and use it to walk to class.

A fifth.

A secret that I'd tried to keep from myself became a secret I needed to keep from my team. My time being "on" the team felt like borrowed time in a place I no longer belonged.

And then, six weeks after my 7:00 AM appointment with the sports psychologist, a doctor looked at my foot and concluded that my injury was "career-ending." Worse: I would likely *always* have pain. As much as I wanted to blame the doctor for forcing me to quit cross country, he really only gave medical language and a bureaucratic mandate to do what I already knew I had to do.

Telling Coach Wilson was deeply unceremonious and humbling. I had already missed the entire indoor season, and outdoor track season had begun, so I had to go and find him on the outdoor track. Behind him, dozens of my teammates were doing what I wanted to be doing. And I had to tell him, through a fence, "I gotta quit."

All he could say was, "Mac," (my nickname), "I love your heart. You gotta do what's right for you. And I gotta get back to practice."

And that was it.

I cleaned up my locker, turned in my gear at the window, and left.

Maybe this sounds melodramatic to you. A story about a young adult letting go of a naive childish fantasy. Heck, it kinda feels that way to even tell that story.

Most people learn to let go of ambitions by the time they become adults. Very few among us have the jobs we fantasized about as children. If we did, the world would have a whole lot more astronauts.

So, yes, you can look at the end of my collegiate cross country career from a safe distance because you weren't there, you're not me, and you probably don't care about cross country as much as I did at 19 years old. But it really was my world. Those feelings were real. I didn't know what alternative existed for me. I had no concept of who I would be without running, so quitting cross country felt like jumping off a cliff into a murky river on a dark and stormy night.

I'm not trying to convince you that I was brave in that moment (although I totally was), I'm illustrating a pattern that people like us fall into when we're passionate and driven. We construct a version of ourselves that's built entirely out of materials we can only find deep, deep inside a belief system, and we forge ahead, using our Awesome like it's the only tool we have. In my case, it was my ability to push people (including myself) as hard as they can go… and sometimes past their limits.

Like I said: people like you and me, we don't "quit." But sometimes we pivot or rebrand.

Doing that? It feels *good*. And like many traps, it has some delicious bait.

Zimas with Jolly Ranchers

I didn't realize how full my arms were until I put down the false belief that I *had* to be a cross country runner.

Suddenly I had hands!

I was able to pay attention to new things. And boy, I did *not* waste any time.

For starters, I realized I was queer, which… look, if you haven't experienced the revelation that comes with realizing your queerness, it's like discovering you've been wearing your clothes inside out and backwards your whole life. ("Ooooh, this is supposed to feel *good*.") It's like learning you've been listening to music with one earbud ("Oh my god… no one told me that this song had *beautiful lyrics*, too!") It's like discovering that bananas are meant to be peeled before eating. ("Wow, why the hell have I been chewing those disgusting peels this whole time?!")

Needless to say, I spent my early 20s making up for lost time.

There was no reason for me to work *so* hard in every single class—I'd always done well in school. No longer held back by my insane habit of trying to anticipate and schedule everything, I had time to take plenty of beautiful and interesting women out. We'd go dancing at the clubs, hit up all sorts of house parties, and drink at the cheap bars on the edge of the campus. I'd order two Zimas, slip a pair of Jolly Ranchers out of my sweaty pockets, and slide them into the bottles.

By ruining a life that wasn't for me, my busted foot had woken me up to what I was missing. I was *grateful*. I'd been spared the futility and embarrassment of wasting all my talent on a dead end path.

It turned out that engaging in dumbassery, just for something to do, was a blast! *Who knew?*

That period of my life can be summed it in one symbol: my Chevy C10, the best vehicle I've ever owned.

I bought it from my ex-boyfriend, Andy, who had used it on his family's farm as a plow truck, an excessive burden on a half-ton pickup truck, poor vehicle. It was a perfect truck for the painting business I was running at the time, because I would literally teach my painters how to spackle by using the rusted out cracks in the body. It was a three on the tree manual transmission, and if I wanted to (and I did want to a lot), I could floor it, take my foot off the gas really, really fast, and it would stall just for a second before making a huge BOOM! Flames would come out of the tailpipe. It was so much fun. Ever since the day I sold it, I have wanted a beater truck in my life.

Anyway, I remember dropping my girlfriend off at her apartment in my Chevy and catching my reflection in the rearview mirror. The scent of her Herbal Essences shampoo lingered, making me swoon. I had a huge, stupid grin on my face, even though tapping the brake pedal shot a quick little jolt of pain through my right foot.

In that truck, while I was having fun, it *hurt to slow down*.

Which suited me just fine, because I've always loved going fast.

My passion was mine to decide what to do with, and I gave it all to my major: architecture.

Immediately, the path came into focus. I would sink my teeth into learning how to design sustainable buildings, and then I would get hired in a firm where I would be able to bring all of my heart and newfound knowledge, making huge changes that influenced the whole industry, while designing gorgeous environments that shone like the Emerald City and ate carbon for breakfast.

Me being me, once I had a direction to go in, I kicked ass at it. When I graduated (with a quite respectable GPA, I might add), I was one of the only graduating seniors with a job offer lined up.

This was especially remarkable, because I was a woman who was absolutely kicking ass in a male-dominated industry.

I stayed on that path until this day, and I have never looked back or changed my mind about anything. I'm living happily ever after! The end!

Nah, I'm messing with you.

This is all still the prologue to my real life's work. My "successes" in architecture turned out *not* to be my happily ever after—far from it.

I succeeded in letting go of a false belief about who I was meant to be (a cross country star) by grabbing hold of a *new* belief about who I might be (the hero of sustainable architecture). And while I won't say I made the wrong choice, I *did* make a similar mistake. Even though I was moving in a different direction, I was still driving a vehicle made out of assumptions and expectations. And I was using a premium kind of fuel: my Awesome.

You have an Awesome, too, dear reader. You know what it's like to go all-in with it. You know what it's like to feel that you owe your Awesome to the world. What you might not recognize is that, while your Awesome enables you to go super fast, you might be using it to go around and around in circles. Going fast is not the same thing as going *far*.

The problem is that, more often than not, pivoting or rebranding doesn't actually mean we're resisting burnout. It means we go through the pains of constructing a whole new version of ourselves, using the materials of a whole other belief system.

It's easy to connect the dots between my being a precocious marching band drummer to destroying my body as a Division 1 athlete to nearly killing myself as a professional architect. My desperate, stubborn, let-everyone-into-your-heart commitment? All I did was redirect it into my academic and professional ambitions in architecture.

Everything in my life looked different, and yet nothing had changed.

Which is how I had a stroke at my desk when I was 31.

Therein lies the first lesson, dear reader: even though you might be making big changes from one phase in your life to the other, those changes can *still* be a part of the same cycle of running balls-out.

Lesson 2

Your safety plan could be the *real* threat to your safety.

SUMMARY: People often try to pacify their fears by making choices that feel "safe." We have theories (which I call "safety plans") about what is supposed to keep us safe. But those theories are often trauma responses. In my case, this happened when my mother mishandled my early exploration of my gender, and I convinced myself I had to follow a safety plan of appearing a certain "acceptable" way in public. If we follow our safety plan and avoid completely falling apart in public, we convince ourselves that this means we're doing okay. When that happens, sometimes our bodies (or other people) mutiny and manufacture burnout to save us from our stubborn minds.

In order to describe what I mean by "safety plan," I need to begin by taking you with me back to my hometown in rural Wisconsin. But this time, we're going even further into the past: 1981.

A muggy, hot summer. Lawn mowers buzzing. A county seat in a damp lowland. Population 3,482.

I'm four years old, and I'm unboxing my first pair of brand-new shoes on the living room floor. My mother brought them home from the Ben Franklin in town.

"What do you think, Laura?" my mom asked.

These shoes represented the absolute pinnacle of personal expression in my short life. They were blue, like I'd asked for, and they had Velcro instead of laces so that I could put them on and take them off all by myself. Now we were talking! I must have been caught up in the excitement of having a pair of shoes, my own pair of shoes, because, even at four years old, I knew that I wanted to protect those shoes from that name.

"Please stop calling me Laura."

Laura is the name my parents gave me at birth, and, needless to say, I've stopped answering to that name. Back then, the only explanation I could give to my bewildered mother was, "It's a girl's name and I don't want it."

"Well, what would you like us to call you?"

"Michael."

My memory has blocked out the exact words she said, but I remember the terror, both hers and mine. The warning: Girls cannot go around in public asking to be called boys' names. Out there in the real world, bad things happen to people like that. You can be who you want to be at home but not out there.

I wonder if she regretted letting me get the blue ones.

After that conversation, Velcroing those shoes felt like defeat. I'd wanted them to belong to Michael. Instead, they came with a cost: keep acting like Laura out in the world.

That conversation made me feel like I was both dangerous and in danger. I would need to pay very close attention to how people perceived me and modulate my gender expression in order to survive and to be accepted. My very first governor, more about that in a minute.

This lesson would become a deep neural pathway that persisted for the next four decades. I carried the secret that who I am is not good. Who I am, at my core, is unsafe and nobody wants to be around it.

There are no corners of my life that lesson didn't touch. This vigilance was present during everything I've already told you about: marching band, cross country, the architecture firm. I "read" everyone in proximity. I was aware of how they perceived me, and I modulated my gender expression so that I would be safe from violence. In some cases, I was probably safer than I realized. In others, I was probably right to be paranoid.

I coped by relentlessly chasing high achievement. In hindsight, I probably figured that if anybody found out that I, the youngest McGinley kid, was queer, at least the record would show that who I am is good, by virtue of my accomplishments. That identity followed me to college and into my early career because I didn't know anything different. I didn't know how to be anyone else.

I adopted the belief that scripts—stories that told me how to be "normal" and "good"—would keep me safe.

Trans people who have spent any time in the closet know all about this, but it affects anyone who feels pressure to conform. When you internalize the belief that you must behave a certain way in order to be accepted, you develop an unconscious obsession. Your mind is constantly on the lookout for threats, telling you how and when to code switch. It hands you a safety plan, and you spend way more energy than you realize trying to obey it.

We think of our minds as being the source of all our intelligence. Our "smarts." Your mind is where your imagination lives. It's the thing that makes us rational, that makes all our conscious decisions. We've thought of our minds as being at the steering wheel of ourselves well before Disney Pixar's Inside Out created the visual metaphor of emotions manning the control panel of our brains.

But our minds can be such dumbasses sometimes.

Which is why someone (or, rather, something) needs to mutiny against our consciousness—or at least provide checks and balances.

That someone? It's your body.

A jagged artifact

Take my stroke as an example. My mind was being such a stupid, abusive dumbass, that my frazzled and depleted body hit the "emergency override" button and hijacked my brain for me in the middle of a typical work day.

If you're not already aware: 31 is FRIGHTENINGLY YOUNG TO HAVE A STROKE. In fact, only about 15% of strokes occur in people under 50 years old.[2] It's wonderful to be a unique and exceptional person, just not in this way!

To paint a picture for you: at that time I was a year-round daily bike commuter, exercised regularly, was nearly vegetarian with a very healthy diet, and stayed hydrated throughout the day. I was the picture of health.

That afternoon, I was at my workstation, using drafting software to complete that day's task, when I noticed that I was having a hard time seeing the screen—despite having 20/20 vision.

I blinked a few times, but it didn't get any better.

I tried closing my eyes for a few seconds, looking away from the screen for a bit. I didn't have *time* for any interruptions. There were designs to submit, a client to call,

---

[2] Centers for Disease Control and Prevention. (n.d.). Stroke facts. CDC. https://www.cdc.gov/stroke/facts.htm

emails that were past-due. But it was still there: a jagged artifact across my vision. Everywhere I looked, there it was.

Then I noticed the headache.

One of my co-workers had been a nurse before she became an architect, and I thought it was a good idea to get her attention. But did I remain seated and call her over? No. Instead, I woozily got up from my chair and staggered across a polished concrete floor. Much as I would have liked to ignore the fact, it was difficult to walk those 100 feet.

"Meredith, I have this jagged thing across my vision and a raging headache that came out of nowhere."

She stood up out of her chair, grabbed both of my shoulders, firmly turned me around, and sat me down in her chair. She looked at me with the clarity and direction that only nurses have and said, "Do not stand up."

At that point, my primary concern was still how on earth I was going to finish my work for the day. Instead, within half an hour, I was checking into the ER, holding my bicycle pannier. I was put in a wheelchair, brought to a room immediately, and the medical professionals went to work on me.

Ugh, now I'll probably have to stay late when I get back.

Those pesky doctors kept fussing over me as though I was some fragile little animal that needed help. Me, the fit-as-hell, grown-ass professional with the bicycle pannier.

Ridiculous.

Little did I know that I would be in the ER for several hours. I tried to convince my co-worker, who had driven me to the hospital, that she should leave, but she refused. (Thank you, Maria.)

The doctor said that the stroke was mild. He didn't have any reason to admit me to the hospital and said I was free to go, but that I should come back immediately if the symptoms returned. At that moment, the only thing I actually heard was that I was not required to stay. In fact, I told him I would just walk home, since the hospital happened to be pretty close to my apartment.

That was a "no ma'am Pam" from both him and Maria.

As Maria wheeled me out of the ER and I prepared to re-emerge into the world, the reality of the situation hit me at once:

Maybe I wasn't invincible.

I'm older and wiser now. Looking back on this memory, I can see the landscape of my life from a different perspective. At 31, I had been hard-headed about following my "safety plan" of high achievement. I was very good at following the plan—but doing so came at a cost. I regularly leveraged adrenaline to accomplish my work tasks.

I believed that my energy was an endless well that I could draw upon to reach my goals. I carried burdens that weren't even *mine* because I was strong enough to do it. I silently suffered. I had very flimsy and permeable boundaries about what I took on. I absorbed everyone's emotions, all the time.

I was totally out of touch with the vast majority of my own emotions.

My safety plan of legitimizing my existence by being an inspiring cross country runner failed to provide the stunt double I needed to avoid breaking my body. When I put that safety plan down, I picked up another one, which exhausted my mind. For the second time in my short life, my safety plan was the thing to kick my ass.

Ambitious pursuits can be a pressure release valve, providing shallow but temporary relief.

Burnout as a spectacle

In popular consciousness, "burnout" is often a dramatic, public spectacle. A star has quite far to fall (Shame! Scrutiny! Humiliation!) when they go from the top (Fame! Admiration! Respect!) to any kind of low (Imperfection! Vulnerability! A subjective opinion about anything!).

Consider the plight of Britney Spears, who, funnily enough, was not able to thread the needle between being a virginal role model and a sex symbol. No wonder she spiraled and buzzed her hair off, given how much the public and media simultaneously antagonized and idolized her.

Mara Wilson (of *Matilda* and *Mrs. Doubtfire* fame) was spared the worst abuses that come with being a former child star because her family helped her make much healthier decisions. But she was close enough to the dangers of fame and popular attention to pen a uniquely empathic defense of

Spears for The New York Times in 2021. She writes, "The saddest thing about Ms. Spears's 'breakdown' is that it never needed to happen… the reality was she was a new mother dealing with major life changes. People need space, time and care to deal with those things. She had none of that."[3]

Space, time, and care.

Britney Spears was denied those things by the media industry, tabloid culture, and the family that exploited her. But it turns out you can utterly destroy your wellbeing just fine without anyone's help.

Your mind is so brilliant and powerful that it can sub in as all three of them. Like an oppressive organization, it can set unrealistic expectations for your work output, denying you the resources you need to be successful. Like a slimy paparazzi reporter, it can judge everything it sees you do and spin your vulnerabilities into cruel, compelling stories. Like a neglectful caregiver, it can exploit and ignore you at the same time.

All of those things can happen without the definitiveness of a spectacular crash. The reason so many of us have a sick fascination with other people's scandals and humiliations is because they permit us to believe we *aren't* burning out. You can convince yourself *you're* okay, *you* weren't photographed by the paparazzi while drunkenly exposing your genitals on

[3] "The Lies Hollywood Tells About Little Girls", The New York Times, Feb. 23, 2021

your way out of a limousine. Or, to use a closer-to-home example: *you're* okay, *you* weren't fired or reprimanded.

The injury of burnout comes from the fact that it's so public. The danger of running balls-out, though, is the fact that it's hidden, or under the cover of plausible deniability.

When you think about it that way, it's quite convenient when our body blows your cover for you.

But it shouldn't have to come to that. Your body's emergency alarm system is not the same thing as a safety plan, and we shouldn't give ourselves permission to rely on it. Imagine using a car's emergency brake at every red light. Yikes. I mean, I haven't tried it, but I know enough about cars to know that the emergency brake is not a one-to-one substitute for the brake pedal.

You need to develop a healthier, more compassionate, more proactive method of self-monitoring so that you can resist a crisis point. And when you receive life-threatening warning signs, you must be prepared to respond with more decisiveness than I was able to.

Because I didn't quit architecture after my stroke. Once again, I only "pivoted."

I failed to see the writing on the wall: that I was chasing a false belief of what I could accomplish as an architect. If I'd been lucid, if I weren't so consumed with ambition, I would have seen that the architects who were pushing the conversation about sustainability were also withering away, not doing well. The ones who were making a ton of money and prizes were surrendering to corporations. The ones who committed themselves to the public good were also spending their brilliant minds figuring out how to hatchet through red tape that had been placed there by the most selfish and vain stakeholders. I wanted to be an architect, but the cost of being one—and not being able to meet my standards for myself—was subsuming my soul.

During those ten years, I worked on initiatives that I am deeply proud of, especially a total renovation of several Minneapolis Public Schools. But in a deeper sense, I was back to running around the track at University of Minnesota, denying the finality of my injury. Withholding from the man in charge that I had already made up my mind to quit the team.

I thought I was running to avoid the Petri Dish of Burnout, but I was actually being dragged closer and closer down into it.

As I'll explain by the end of this book, avoiding the Petri Dish of Burnout and honoring your life's work requires you to do things differently. It requires you to confront the thing that scares you most. It requires a commitment that doesn't occur in a way that is comfortable or gradual. Yep, it's gonna feel like the harsh slap of cold when you plunge into a river butt naked.

It's kind of amazing.

Lesson 3

You can really frack yourself up when you work in sustainability.

SUMMARY: There are systemic reasons why working in climate is harder, which are directly tied to dominant ideas about what leadership means, which are reinforced by the corrupt, powerful men who have amassed power throughout history. Being a leader in a more compassionate way requires you to unlearn those dominant ideas. It takes intense discipline and is nearly impossible to do on your own. When I tried to balance it with my work, I ran balls-out every hour of every day. It was going to take me forever. But, after hiring a coach and becoming a guide for other people, I learned that burnout has an opposite, which is just as powerful.

As a young adult, all the beliefs I had about leadership had centered around one particular style of leadership. You know the style: using brute force and proselytization in order to bend other people to your will. The guy who got to be leader was the one who could prove that he was the toughest and loudest and meanest dude in the room.

But over time I learned that leadership could look like something else. That it was possible to lead with heart.

Our traditional image of leadership-by-brute-force feels bad, isn't healthy, and—worst of all—it doesn't work. Sure, you can "win" that way. Sure, you can access power. It might even feel like you're in control. But that way of wielding influence is hollow and unsustainable. It's empty carbs, and while it can feel like it's filling you, it's just gonna pass right through your system without providing any actual nutritional value. Worse, it'll frustrate you and compel you to consume and extract more, causing harm and destruction on your path to more power.

Leadership-by-brute-force is one of several direct routes to burnout.

Actual leadership, the kind that comes from the heart, involves humility. Changing your mind. Trusting and empowering a team. Learning new information. Relinquishing control. Balancing internal and external work. Pausing, processing, practicing. Facing fears. Embracing vulnerability.

If that sounds like a lot of extra work, that's because it is. But obviously that kind of leadership requires extra work; it's an act of love. And love means putting in the extra work.

The rewards are profound, and well worth the effort. Compassionate leadership creates movements that are larger than any one person's ego. They exist outside a single person—that's what makes those movements viable and durable. Leading with love yields regenerative and autonomous movements that don't need to suck the life force out of anyone in order to stay alive, and don't rely on a cult of personality.

Leading by heart is the only sustainable form of leadership. And I mean that in multiple senses of the word: emotional sustainability as well as planetary. Check out how many double meanings there are here:

Leaders who care about their own wellbeing and the wellbeing of everyone on their team make sure that their initiatives run on renewable emotional energy—just like leaders who love the planet make sure their technology runs on renewable energy.

They create a healthy work climate and look for ways to positively impact the environment. They recognize that the healthiest approaches come from being emotionally authentic, present, and organic, instead of relying on generic niceties that might look prettier but are ultimately artificial.

You get the point.

And, yes, this analogy is kinda corny, but remember that it was the loudest, pushiest dudes who created the systems that made us reliant on fossil fuels, who are responsible for spewing toxins in our water and air, who waged wars in order to consolidate wealth and insulate their egos. It's no coincidence that, to a man, each of their "leadership" styles rely on fear, submission, and fealty to one strongman and his grievances. (That's why it's often traumatic for those movements when their leader dies.)

The most insidious thing about those strongmen is that so many people believe their story of what "leadership" should look like, even though giving them power is literally destroying the planet. They've convinced just about everyone that we should try to be like them. That the only way to be successful is to be at their service. Like all bullies, strongmen change the rules of the game to suit them.

More and more people are being impacted by the consequences of their greed and short-sightedness. Even conservative projections estimate that 200 million people will be displaced by climate change and/or global conflict by the year 2050.[4] (That's the whole country of Bangladesh plus some or two-thirds of the population of the United States.) Meanwhile, the strongmen have made it so that the cards have been stacked against qualities like compassion, attentiveness, rest, moderation, and trust. This is a major reason we're living in a period of paranoia, distrust, and social isolation.

But this upswell of toxic assholery we're seeing right now? That's their attempt to wrest control of the global narrative, because the increasing societal concern and

---

4 World Bank. 2021. Groundswell Part 2: Acting on Internal Climate Migration. World Bank. https://www.worldbank.org/en/news/press-release/2021/09/13/climate-change-could-force-216-million-people-to-migrate-within-their-own-countries-by-2050

awareness of climate change is threatening to take control away from them. They're scared.

I don't bring this up because I'm trying to scare you, I bring it up because now is our chance to figure out how to remake the entire world using your Awesome. Look, you're on the other side of this whole I'm-writing-a-book-that-you're-reading divide, so I don't know who you are or what your Awesome is. But I do know that your Awesome isn't your desire for fame, wealth, and power. It's something related to your capacity for love.

It's your willingness to do what is right instead of what's easy (to paraphrase the headmaster of a certain magical school of witchcraft and wizardry).

Swimming against the tide—and knowing how to do so in industries that were constructed to prevent you from doing so—requires struggle, resolve, risk, introspection, and a ton of resistance. Yes, resistance: from the safety plans that were written to control us, not to protect us.

Even when we consciously understand that we want to resist, knowing how to do so is often completely unintuitive to us because it goes so explicitly against how we were taught to be in the world.

You are capable of doing that, but interrupting patterns is seriously hard to do on one's own.

The Christmas hoarder

Here's a low-stakes example:

My friend Linda used to have way too many Christmas decorations. Whatever you're picturing, it was worse. Her garage, her attic, her basement, her storage unit... every single one of them was filled, floor to ceiling, with plastic bins.

To be fair, they were labeled: *Stockings. Ornaments. Nutcrackers. Animated animals. More animated animals. Still more animated animals.*

Her kids were all grown up and moved out; it wasn't like she was hosting Christmas anymore. But she still hadn't gotten rid of the relics of her holiday-hosting past. "None of these animated animals even work anymore!" she admitted, kind of laughing at herself.

I didn't have to ask her if she was planning on getting rid of all the junk she wasn't using anymore. She could see it in my eyes. I cared about her, so I worried. At best, all the clutter was useless. At worst, it was a constant reminder of an idealized past she hadn't yet let go of.

"I'm working on it," she'd assure me, "bit by bit."

To her credit, this was technically true. One year, she bragged that she'd donated a box of old baby onesies to a hospital. The next, she'd gifted a bunch of nutcrackers to the Ukrainian woman down the block.

"That's great," I'd say, but I'd be doing the mental math. If she kept up this rate of one box every few months, she'd finish up around… multiply by 12… carry the 9… 2 turtle doves and…

approximately at the same time that the sun is expected to swallow the Earth.

I want you to try and imagine what Linda's floor-to-ceiling, wall-to-wall bins of wrapping paper look like when I say to you:

You are *fully capable* of accessing the fully realized power of your Awesome on your own. But *it will take forfuckingever.* And taking forever to commit your Awesome to the world's challenges is not sustainable. And it robs us of your Awesome.

Now, the story of Linda's Christmas decorations has a happy ending. When she and her husband retired and decided to relocate closer to their kids, some of her friends generously came over and forced the issue.

They dealt with it methodically. There was a yard sale involved. A caravan of donations. A shameful amount of stuff went to the landfill. Linda was allowed one extremely exclusive "keep" pile, which went with her to North Carolina.

Linda might have eventually reached the back of her attic on her own, but it could not have happened within her lifetime without a sense of urgency *and* the support of other people who could provide tough love and objective accountability. Plus, she would be perpetually haunted by the pressure of an un-dealt-with problem.

But enough about Linda. Back to young architect me.

"Something's gotta change," I told myself, while feeling deeply limited and exhausted by my work in architecture.

So I bought a bunch of books.

I read about different approaches to architecture and explored other kinds of working opportunities. I tried out teaching to see if that felt any less awful.

"What if I do this instead?" I asked. I tried about a million things instead, and they were each their own unique flavor of frustrating because I still hadn't radically influenced the field of architecture, and *shouldn't I be able to given how awesome I know I am?!*

I tried everything in the world except actually facing my fears. The new approaches piled up on top of my false belief, not instead of it.

I understood that I had a pattern to break, but I was only gradually peeling away at the corners of the problem, like the sticky, stubborn paper label on a bottle of beer. The process was painstakingly slow and unsatisfying.

I was limited by my own self-awareness.

But I've gotta tell you, when I look back on this period today, I can honestly tell you that I think to myself: *What a gift.*

All of it. The pain and everything. What a gift. I'm so glad that my cross country career fell apart at 19, instead of 29 or 39 or whenever. That I didn't march forward doing the amount of exercise I would have needed to in order to keep being a runner, which I totally could have. That kind of thing doesn't happen for a lot of runners until they're in their 30s or 40s.

Hitting rock bottom with my pursuits as an architect was similar. Even though I didn't have an injury, I was emotionally struggling enough that my body created a kind of injury *for* me.

After two trysts with burnout, I tried to fix it on my own—by trying to "fix" my career in architecture.

When dream jobs become nightmares

I left the firm to teach, and while I was teaching, I picked up a side hustle that turned into a dream job: Head of Education, Sales, and Product Development for a startup that was using mass timber products to replace steel and concrete. Super ideal! I got to go into architecture offices and teach people about the product and help them navigate the code quagmire to get it specified. I got to develop new products that I really believed in. I got to lead and mentor a team of drafters. I got to be creative. I got to be a part of shaping the *future*.

But I was still me. I went about it with an unsustainable attitude, and got swept up in the breakneck speed of the company culture. They asked so much of us, and I didn't have the right boundaries yet. I had achieved everything that I had worked towards and I was making good money, but it was 10-12 hour days, six days a week plus travel. There was no balance in it. At the time, my wife and I had a three-year-old and a newborn in a house that we were actively renovating. I couldn't afford for all of my physical symptoms of burnout to return.

While I stand by the vision and values I brought to my work in architecture, I can't honestly say I moved the needle on climate as an architect. The most I was able to accomplish was in my capacity as an owner's representative for Minneapolis Public Schools, where I got to influence the decision of the mechanicals that went into the building based on their efficiency and efficacy, and on the materials that went in and their circularity (or lack thereof). But that's about it.

I knew that the world was full of wisdom I could access and borrow in order to get me out of this quagmire, and, armed with my library card, I went looking for it.

I used my free time to read about business economics from the 1920s and squinted past all the oil baron bullshit. I read about self-esteem and personal branding. About mysticism, psychology, personality types, leadership, and much more.

This was a period in my life when I was a stress puppy all day long, running balls-out at work, eating dinner standing up, renovating my house until 10:00 pm, then taking a shower with the backyard hose because the bathroom was offline. I spent every weekend working on renovations. Consequently, "reading in my free time" looked like lying down in bed and passing out after reading a sentence or two.

Needless to say, it took me *forever* to read each book. With each one, I'd lose the arc of the book by the time I got to the end.

In a messed up way, it was euphoric in the same way running balls-out is. It's addictive, and you can do it for a while, but not forever. But this time I was more prepared to deal with it. There didn't need to be a stroke event to snap me out of it, just an unsustainable new baseline of feeling constantly pissed. Even though there wasn't a doctor this time to tell me, "Stop running, dumb-dumb, you need to wear a walking cast," I had myself and my wife to tell me, "You're in trouble, dude."

My world fell apart again, making it abundantly clear that I couldn't go on like this. I didn't get fired and the startup job wasn't excessed. I *chose* to leave and try another way to deal with my issues—on my own. It took a while for me to realize that trying to do it alone wasn't working.

It wasn't until I had the support of David, my first coach, that I was able to actually change my perspective and commit to my life's work in a much realer way: by *putting down the script* and becoming comfortable acting without one. I needed for someone else to catalyze and accelerate the work I had to do to use my Awesome responsibly. It felt amazing to finally be making progress on my goals, experiencing growth, and facing my demons head on. Somehow, it felt like I was both *returning* to myself and *becoming* myself.

For the first time since I obediently put on my blue Velcro sneakers, I stopped depending on my safety plan. I learned how to distinguish fear from peril, and to pay attention to the information that my body and environment were providing to me.

All that eventually led me to the place where I am today, where I'm able to encourage and uplift people, apply my knowledge, and embody my values.

So of course, in hindsight, I look back on it and I say:

What a gift.

I got to be like Linda, enjoying a sip of hot chocolate in her spacious new house in North Carolina, realizing that she was finally able to feel the spirit of her favorite holiday after letting go of the junk pile she'd created as a hollow tribute to it.

Yes, a gift. Honestly, truly.

Although, was the detour of nearly *dying* completely necessary?

It was nice arriving in a state of self-actualization and all, but does every journey of growth *have* to involve a scenic route (or three) through rock bottom? Those experiences made me the person I was becoming, and I happen to be a pretty big fan of that person, but had I missed a shortcut or something?

If I *had*, would taking that shortcut have actually gotten me to the same place? Would I have arrived there being less fully-baked and more ill-equipped?

Of course, this was one of those pointless meditations; none of us can change the past. But I was so frustrated by my wasted time and energy, my needless suffering and trauma, and I needed to do something about it.

David suggested to me about a million times that I would be an excellent coach, but I was stubbornly holding onto my identity as an architect.

Something about the coaching space creeped me out. There were all these tech bros promising each other wealth and fame, beige-clad women promising each other the time to do yoga, hipsters promising a more balanced lifestyle and artistic freedom. Promises, assurances, guarantees—"or your money back!" They had formulas. Frameworks. E-courses. The best way. The only way. The proven way. The *easy* way.

It felt like they were promising a kind of salvation—a return to normalcy. A quick fix for achieving what you always wanted to achieve.

I didn't want to yuck anyone's yum, but what irked me was this sense that it's in everyone's best interest to accomplish exactly what they've always wanted. The problem I saw was that, more often than not, there are deeper, more important problems than not getting what you want, like what we do to *get* it. There's the problem of holding on too stubbornly to a goal that isn't serving us. There's the problem of remaining dissatisfied, even when we accomplish our supposed goals (and when the things we want nearly kill us).

The healing we need as people rarely comes from having the solutions to the problems we're aware we have, or the answers to the questions we know how to ask.

Obviously, I don't want to see people suffer. I wanted to spare people the worst of what I'd been through. But something told me that my calling wasn't to help people *avoid* difficulty. It was to help them *through* difficulty, and to take something meaningful from it. It was to help us make the active choices necessary in order for our work in sustainability to be sustainable for our hearts, minds, and bodies.

That doesn't happen automatically.

You have to choose it.

For most of us, that requires nothing less of us than to confront our greatest fears. "That doesn't sound like a coach," I tried to explain to David. "Coaches blow whistles and tell people what to do and how to do it. I'm more of a *guide*."

"That's fine," David replied. "So be a guide."

The alternative force

I know you don't *want* to run balls-out. You don't want to completely deplete your body and spirit, or be a part of a work culture of constant panic and abuse. When you're pushing forward with passion and care, you're an unstoppable force—but an even more *powerful* force is likely to shove you off your current trajectory.

I used to think that burnout was the only force powerful enough (outside of death) to really impact the momentum of someone like you, with Awesome to spare, who is on a mission. I saw how burnout could steer a person towards growth, balance, and healing like it did for me.

But there's a second force, in addition to burnout, that can have the same effect. That second force is what I believe to be the *opposite* of burnout. A better option, one that I hadn't known to search for. Like burnout, it can knock you off your stubborn descent down a destructive path. But *unlike* burnout, it serves to preserve, strengthen, and unleash the power of your Awesome.

In order to really describe that second force, though, I need to take us to a place where we can look down directly into the Petri Dish of Burnout itself. Because understanding the way to avoid the Petri Dish requires us to understand the many different ways that smart, talented people wind up in there.

So:

Let's go.

Yup, you and me.

Right now.

We're going on a run.

Tie this rope around your waist.

Section 2

Four laps

Intro

For the next little while (a.k.a. section 2 of this book), we're gonna run a couple laps. It's a slightly dangerous trail, but we're in the best possible company. Remember that cross country exercise I told you about? The one I did with my team back in rural Wisconsin? We are running as a team, tethered to a big loop.

There's a few other amazing people running on our team, and each of them will help you get through this.

It takes a certain kind of person to decide to be on this team. You have to be absolutely insanely passionate and driven in order to do something as crazy as tie a rope around your waist and run across a slippery, slanted track.

Did I forget to mention that the track is slippery and slanted? Oh, uh… yeah, the track is slippery and slanted.

As a matter of fact, we're running along the inside of a giant funnel.

But trust me, you are going to be safe.

As we start running, it's going to become immediately clear that this run will be awkward and exhausting, but our group isn't going to let that stop us. We'll adjust our gait, accommodate for that weird angle, and forge ahead through the pain.

You might be wondering if this path will even out eventually.

I'm afraid not. Our running path is a loop entirely inside this giant funnel.

In the middle of this giant loop, there's a sudden and sharp drop. And—don't go to the ledge to look, just take my word for it—at the bottom of that drop is the namesake of this book: the Petri Dish of Burnout.

Ah yes, the Petri Dish of Burnout. Normal petri dishes are tiny, you can hold them in the palm of your hand. But the Petri Dish of Burnout defies physics. The closer you get, the bigger it gets, until The Petri Dish of Burnout is holding *you*.

The Petri Dish is where good ideas and great potential go to rot. It's a writhing, steaming clump that looks like a single organism, but if you squint, you'll see that it's actually several. It's hard to tell the difference between which of these life forms have given up, and which are continuing to sputter futilely, but it doesn't matter, because the effect is the same: this big clump consumes energy, and it doesn't even do anything productive with it.

As I told you in section one, I've been in the Petri Dish a time or two. Landing in there was so terrible and pointless (and it took forever to wash off the stink), but that rough landing was what it took for me to turn my life around.

If any one of us falls into the Petri Dish, the rest of us are going to get dragged down with them.

So let's go back to the question I posed in the last section: is all this necessary? Do we *need* to run through the Petri Dish of Burnout in order to emerge, on the other side, in a better place? A place where we don't have to be balls-out about everything? Is the Petri Dish a fountain of knowledge we *must* drink from?

I have an answer to that question but, believe it or not, that answer isn't exactly straightforward. It's not a simple "yes" or "no." It depends on your definition of burnout. It may look like subconsciously sabotaging yourself or subsuming your needs and biting your tongue. It may mean succeeding spectacularly at the cost of everything important to you. It may even mean alienating everyone around you and blaming them for the divorce. Whatever it is, it's not the thing you were born to do, and it's not helping the world.

To get at what really matters at the heart of the question, I need to get specific. I need to tell you about the four different types of ambitious leaders who are most often drawn to healing the world. I'll describe how each of them are basically programmed to crash and burn spectacularly, but also how they each can use basic mindfulness and reflection tactics in order to find balance and access their Awesome. Yes, I need to tell you about all four of them, because we lose really important insights by lumping them into one monolithic idea of what burnout "is," what causes it, and how to address it. Burnout isn't one story, it's many chaotic choose-your-own-adventure scenarios.

The four types of ambitious leaders I'm talking about are Perfectionists, Heroes, Researchers, and Motivators. These "types" are defined by the key ways that they perceive the world and their role in it. None of these are good guys or bad guys, okay? These aren't Hogwarts houses with the supposedly all-evil Slytherins. All four types are amazing and wonderful, and we need every single one of them (and also folks who aren't ambitious leaders) in order to create the tomorrow we need.

Knowing that there are multiple styles of burnout gives us better questions than "is burnout necessary?" Questions like, is it possible for a Perfectionist to embrace subjectivity without a crisis of faith? Can a Hero save other people without martyring themselves? What is necessary for a Researcher to integrate uncertainty into their worldview? Can a Motivator give up control without a massive power struggle?

To explore those questions, I'm going to tell you four stories each about a character who is an idealized version of each type. I'm describing them like real people, because we tend to respond more to the nuances of other humans in stories in ways that we don't respond to narrative descriptions of categories. After all, people binge Netflix dramas in a way they don't binge books about Myers–Briggs.

Olive, Trip, Fiona, and Eisen are characterized in ways that are hyper-specific—down to their ability to maintain eye contact—because the differences between these types of leaders is often a matter of what it's like to be with them. I want you to notice when these stories remind you of yourself and of the ambitious leaders in your life. Keep your ears open for echoes.

Does Eisen's approach to conflict remind you of your brother's?

Does your company's CEO have some of Fiona's tendencies?

Does Olive's bedtime routine remind you of your own?

See if you can recognize key people in your life in at least two of the characters. The journey into (and out of) the Petri Dish of Burnout is best understood when you're able to see how the routes are both different from and similar to each other for each type.

You'll see what I mean.

Let's start with *her*, the one towards the front of our team, pushing herself harder than anyone else. The woman whose cheeks are red with effort. Her running outfit looks fantastic. Is it possible that she *ironed* it this morning?

She's muttering a lot under her breath. Self-conscious about her gait. Comparing her speed to everyone else's. Worrying about the slope of this hill.

"Crap," she whispers, as soon as someone else passes her.

She notices that one of her shoelaces is tied more floppily than the other. Her eyes bug out. She scans around to see if anyone notices.

She keeps glancing down at them.

She does it so much that she misses the bump in the path and trips over it, jostling the rest of our party, and distracting them.

"Sorry, guys."

She notices a funny feeling on her lower back. Goodness forbid: the waistband of her shorts is twisted in one spot.

Quickly, her hands rustle to fix it, her elbows akimbo, bumping into the people around her. More distraction. More apologies.

Then, she notices the tag sticking out in the back of one of our teammate's shirts.

"Psst," she says. "Hey!"

Confused glances. No one knows who she's talking to, or what's so important that it needs to be talked about while we're all out of breath. People start bumping into each other.

"Your shirt tag!" she warns the guy in front of her.

"It doesn't matter!" he huffs back.

We continue running. But all she can look at is the shirt tag.

This is Olive, the Perfectionist.

Lesson 4

Perfectionism can be a form of avoidance (the Olive lesson).

SUMMARY: Olive represents the Perfectionist archetype. She has a remarkable eye for detail and high standards for her development work at a climate action nonprofit. But her inner critic (which I imagine as a gremlin on her shoulder named Evilo) sows doubt and keeps her awake at night. To counter this, Olive adapted her approach to fundraising calls to give her more breathing room, to allow for meaningful observation and connection. To help with this, I recommend that Perfectionists (and everyone else) try a mindfulness exercise called Balloon Breath (page 86).

Olive took meetings in the hoity-toity coworking space where her company rented out a small office. One of those places that felt like it was legally required to carry kombucha on tap. Hipsters with headphones and laptops, tech bros in gaggles of three and four women in knitted gray sweaters and Lululemon leggings.

Olive wasn't dressed the fanciest, but she was dressed the best. And, as she selected a booth to settle into, she offered hello's and hi's to this and that person. It felt a bit like she was running for mayor of the co-working community.

"Hey Martin, congrats on the product launch! How did it go?" she asked one guy. He gave her a thumbs up and continued on his way out of the café.

"Crap," she whispered under her breath, "it wasn't a product launch, it was a rebrand." Not that Martin seemed to notice. But she swallowed down the shame and retrieved a clean new notebook and a fancy new pen from her classy little briefcase. A click of the pen, a swish of straight blond hair, a suppressed yawn. "All right, let's get started."

You might be a Perfectionist if:

- Your idea of a wild night is reorganizing your sock drawer by color and fabric type.

- Your inner critic has its own inner critic.

- You have a "right way" to load the dishwasher—and a presentation to prove it.

- You've noticed crooked picture frames in a stranger's house and have not been able to stop thinking about it.

- You carry a mini lint roller in your car... just in case.

- You've rephrased someone's compliment to make it more accurate.

- Your definition of fun includes making a to-do list— and then checking off "make a to-do list."

- You've apologized to an inanimate object for bumping into it.

- You secretly enjoy editing your friends' texts for grammar and punctuation.

- You have a hard time making big changes because that would mean admitting that you were wrong in the past.

- You believe in spontaneous fun, as long as it's scheduled between 2:00 and 2:15 p.m.

- You correct people's pronunciations in your head... and then have a hard time listening to the rest of their sentences.

Olive's perfect pitch

Olive hired me because she wanted to get her act together in time for a fundraising deadline. "I'm only 47% of the way to my goal and there are only two months to go. I need to figure out what I'm doing wrong on these calls and fix it."

At 32 years old, Olive was the director of development for a local climate action nonprofit. She'd spent her post-college years kicking ass fundraising for private charities. Before college, she'd earned a Girl Scout Gold Award by raising $25,000 for her church. Fundraising had always been her *thing*, and she was very good at it.

She keeps recordings of most of her fundraising calls (having received consent from all parties, of course). Olive's smile is big and bright. Her voice is loud and clear. Her outfit and hair are neat and tidy.

Her background is blurred out.

She slips in compliments about the recent work of a prospective donor. She highlights recent work that her own nonprofit has done. She alludes to upcoming events.

She maneuvers, efficiently, through a predetermined agenda.

The people she talks to nod politely. They answer her questions. They ask their own questions at three prescribed moments.

They are along for the ride, keeping their arms and legs inside the vehicle, so to speak.

The calls all have a clear beginning, middle, end, and call to action—because that's how the template she wrote for herself flows.

In other words, she followed the protocol perfectly every time. But she noticed that two things weren't working for her: 1) fewer and fewer people were interested in contributing or investing in the non-profit, and 2) she was increasingly critical of herself.

She came to me because she hoped I could help her learn what language to use when talking to folks in climate. She wanted to be more creative, to figure out some new approaches. "Like, if I'm able to get on a call with someone from the Bezos Earth Fund... I can't mess that up. Did you get a new haircut?"

Huh?

Oh, she was talking to one of the gray-sweater-yoga-ladies.

"Oh, it's a new *color*. It looks *awesome!*" she said to her. And then, to herself a moment later, "I don't know where my head's at." More self-flagellation.

She had deep, dark circles under her eyes. "Truth be told, this fundraising deadline is kind of make-or-break for the company. This is why they hired me. This is what I'm good at. And for some reason I can't seem to get through to these people. Part of it is that the climate world is new to me." She sighed. "And part of it is that I'm just plain *tired*."

Of course she was tired. Olive sets her alarm to 5:00 a.m. to get her stretching routine and PT exercises in. Then, she wakes up the kids (twins in elementary school). She makes sure everyone eats breakfast, gives her husband a pep talk and a sandwich, and gets out the door on time. She drops the kids off at school, then drives her EV to the co-working space. She spends most of her day either on calls with potential donors or researching them.

Her husband is a lawyer. They live in a trendy and desirable neighborhood nearby, and her sister comes around to help with the kids a few days of the week. She coordinates multiple color-coded paper calendars in the house. In short: she has help, but she stage-manages the household.

"The kids are in bed by 8:00. Roger and I alternate who reads them bedtime stories. We always have an hour-long TV show, so we watch that. In bed, because he always passes out. Then I do my hair and skincare routine and get back in bed."

When I met her, Olive was in the habit of bringing her phone into bed to close out her email and Slack threads. "And yeah, I doom scroll a little. I text my cousins, my friends." Pause. "And I always have tabs open. Articles I need to read." Pause. "But I'm getting better at adding things to my to-do list for the next day."

Her rule was that she had to turn off her lamp and shut her eyes at 10:00, but it took quite a while longer for her to actually fall asleep.

This is the case for a lot of Perfectionists, actually. Here's why.

The inner critic

Perfectionists like Olive have a fierce inner critic. An unsparing, jerky little gremlin who shows up to torment her *the very second she's left alone without a distraction.*

Olive dreaded shutting her lamp off at 10:00 every night, because her lights-out time was her inner critic's playground. He cranked up the volume, picked up the mic, and started the Olive bash—and it really was a *bash*. He had a playlist with all the top 40 hits: the everything-you-did-wrong-today salsa. The everything-you're-gonna-mess-up-tomorrow disco. The everyone-is-judging-you country ballad. The you-don't-deserve-nice-things R&B number. The it's-just-a-matter-of-time-before-you-die-alone original Broadway cast recording featuring Idina Menzel.

Until Olive dealt with that inner critic, she would continue to lie awake at night, seduced by his cruelty.

Let's call the inner critic Evilo—Olive spelled backwards.

Making the situation more complicated was that Olive was extremely open to constructive criticism and direct feedback. In fact, she asked for it all the time. And when she received it, Olive would listen carefully, but so would Evilo. Oh, he'd lick his lips at every bit of my feedback, no matter how carefully and compassionately it was delivered. As soon as Olive heard it, Evilo would be coming up with messed up ways of remixing it:

"Consider Turning Off Your Blur Filter" (You Cold, Standoff-ish Weirdo edition)

"You Seem So Polished" (Which is Why Everyone Secretly Hates You version)

"You Look Great Today" (featuring Self-deprecating Downward Spiral)

Evilo is brilliant. He can turn any feedback Olive receives about her work into an insult. Eleanor Roosevelt once said, "No one can make you feel inferior with your consent," but she didn't know Evilo. Evilo is the part of Olive that *does* consent to feeling inferior. Doing so gives him a schadenfreude thrill.

That's why Olive surrounded herself with other people. With routines. With smartphone notifications. With obligations. All of these things kept her inner critic at bay, but only temporarily. Olive was running, balls-out, away from the taunts of Evilo, which has the same effect of being controlled by him.

She needed a different soundtrack to listen to in those moments where she was alone with herself. If Evilo was going to make a playlist that discouraged her, killed joy, and presented obstacles—Olive needed to make one that *encouraged* her, *created* joy, and presented *opportunities*.

In order to do that, she re-designed the template—for her bedtime routine.

Instead of concluding the day focused on her sense of obligation to others, she picked up a favorite hobby and did something for herself—by knitting a scarf.

She'd used to knit things for the twins when they were babies, but hadn't touched her yarn stash in years. On her phone, she had pictures of a matching pair of knitted jumpers that she made for both of the kids (adorable), an afghan she crafted for her sister for her wedding (very geometrically pleasing), a gorgeous colorwork scarf for her husband (super impressive), and more. She seemed to blush a bit at "bragging." Of course, she could quickly point out what was "wrong" with each of them—a cable that went in the wrong direction, a color that didn't match, a dropped stitch in a pant leg... nothing I could perceive.

By redirecting her care and meticulousness towards a pleasurable project of self-reverence, Olive grabbed the mic from her inner critic and belted her own favorite tunes.

"I Deserve Yarn This Soft"

"Another Row For Me"

"(I'm Gonna Look So Fine) In This Scarf"

The world needs you, Perfectionist, because:

- You bring order to chaos with your meticulous systems.

- You identify flaws and work tirelessly to correct them, transforming challenges into opportunities for growth.

- You uphold high standards, refusing to settle for mediocrity and inspiring others to strive for excellence.

- You understand that the details matter.

- You act with integrity, doing what's right even when no one is watching, and in doing so, set a powerful example for others.

- You are the unsung hero of accuracy.

- You are a highly principled individual with a strong sense of right and wrong. You remind us that integrity is more than a concept—it's a way of life that leads to authentic success.

- You address overlooked issues.

- You remind us that improvement is always possible.

- You hold the moral compass steady, providing guidance and clarity when the world wavers.

- You inspire us to be better, not just for ourselves, but for the greater good, leading by example in pursuit of a brighter future.

Putting down the script

Olive and I met for a few months, and yes, we also talked about her work directly. We worked on her fundraising calls like she asked. Perfectionists like to have things they can tinker with, so we worked on the standard operating procedure that she had developed. Like I expected, it was a script with blank spots like a Mad Libs book.

"We've all been really inspired by what you and your team are doing! [Refer to a specific picture from their most recent event.] It's one of the many reasons we're so glad to be community partners with you."

"Since you're interested in [choose key theme from their mission statement], do you mind if I tell you about some upcoming events on our calendar?"

"The last time I saw you was at the [insert event here], and I've been thinking about the [insert anecdote here]."

Olive decided to rewrite and restructure her call template into a looser and sparser set of recommendations. Less a script and more a toolbox of prompts. Less minute-by-minute and more à la carte.

Soon, the first instruction on the SOP was the extremely up-for-interpretation "address personal connections for about 10 minutes, then pivot with something like *shall we dive in?*"

Over time, Olive became more naturally improvisational, letting her guard down and her hair down (so to speak). Eventually, someone spotted the yarn behind Olive and asked her what she was knitting. "We got totally derailed," she said about the incident. "We wound up talking about knitting for about 20 minutes, and then her company decided to take out an ad for one of our events."

It wasn't just knitters, though. Someone else spotted a book he loved on a shelf, and Olive wound up exchanging book recommendations with him. His company became a co-sponsor for an event.

"I keep not getting through the whole agenda," Olive admitted, "but it doesn't seem to matter. People donate anyway."

Of course they did. Now they were meeting with a person who was capable of engaging sincerely with them while, in her endearing way, directing the conversation tactfully and actively. She started taking more risks. She expressed more emotions. She even took more credit for her personal contributions to different facets of the company. A sense of pride started to shine through.

She had ceased trying to engineer the perfect call, and became able to have a *good* one.

Once she was able to stop apologizing for getting off track ("Sorry, I'm rambling!"), more and more of her calls turned into a positive experience. Even if the person on the other end didn't choose to donate, Olive was able to identify reasons why, which weren't her own "flaws."

"Things are really tight in that sector right now." "They committed to donating more to women-owned organizations, so I flagged them for if I ever branch out on my own." "Honestly, it just wasn't a match—and come to think of it, our board wouldn't want us to be seen taking money from them."

The week Olive bound off her scarf and started wearing it happened to be the same time she had a call scheduled with the director of giving from the Bezos Earth Fund. Naturally, she was very nervous. She considered going back to her scripted approach, as though her joyful improvised approach was acceptable for netting "small fish," but a "white whale" like the Bezos Earth Fund was too prestigious for indulgences like her joy, personality, and passion. In short, for her scarf.

She decided to wear it anyway.

And the call didn't go well.

The rep she spoke to was stiff and impatient. He didn't want to engage. Olive tried to pivot to a more stoic, organized level of engaging. It felt like too little too late. She got self-conscious. She stuttered and sputtered and even her very familiar script wasn't a firm enough anchor to stabilize her in such a disorienting moment. As she hung up, she knew, beyond a shadow of a doubt, that it was going to be a "no."

The next day wasn't pretty.

Olive did what she always did when she was in a dark mood: she threw herself into work. She showed up at her desk early, created accounts on the three best hiring platforms available, and set out to hire a better sales rep.

"I think I realized that I know how to develop a good messaging strategy, but a good fundraiser has to be more natural and comfortable and intuitive than I am to be having the actual conversations with these people, and I can't even do that without constantly having to build and rebuild frameworks to have any semblance of executive functioning."

As she surveyed the headlines of a few of the applicants, Evilo was laughing his butt off. Just as Olive was developing her way of approaching fundraising calls from a place of greater authenticity, he had somehow persuaded her that because it hadn't worked with one (albeit important) audience member, she was now disqualified from doing the thing in the world that she's best at. Evilo told Olive that she was a liability. That she needed to protect the company from her own flaws. That who she is was bad.

But then she shut her eyes.

And she took a deep breath.

Try This: Balloon Breath

For the longest time, I thought breathing exercises and other mindfulness practices were kinda bullshit.

Then, I tried it for myself. I quickly realized that they super aren't, they've just been commodified beyond recognition.

Balloon Breath is a guided meditation focused on the breath and bringing your attention inward. (You have to be able to hear it in order to follow along, so go download it from book.vialucent.com) It starts by simply noticing your natural breathing, then encourages you to slow down the exhale and pause briefly. The main part of the exercise involves visualizing an internal balloon that you inflate with your breath, which helps to draw your focus and energy back into your body. The goal is to create a sense of being present and connected to yourself, without any pressure or judgment.

- Use this when you're aware that you're feeling drained or your attention is too focused on other people or other things.

- Use this breath to recharge your battery.

- Use this to get to a quiet place, so that you can hear what your heart is whispering to you.

- Use this breath to break a habit of constantly reading everyone who is around you.

- Use this breath to feel more like *you*.

It's a safe and rewarding practice that can become easier with repetition.

In fact, the real power in this exercise comes from doing it more than once. The more you do it, the more you'll get out of it. Your heart is constantly whispering vital wisdom, but the noise of the world is usually too loud for us to be able to hear it. By creating space between yourself and the many external interests and forces that are commanding your attention, **you will become able to hear what your heart is whispering to you.**

Segue

We're back on the running track.

Olive is so committed to our team that she would almost rather subsume herself than feel responsible for holding us back. The amount of energy she is spending tinkering, micromanaging, and worrying is exhausting her. If she fell behind, she'd drag us all behind, too. Which would break her heart, and make her even more discouraged and ashamed. That would mean we get pulled backwards, get knocked off balance, and dragged to the ground, where we'd become a tangle of confused limbs, and fall, slowly and inevitably, into the Petri Dish of Burnout.

But that's not happening, because Olive is about to make a different choice.

Let's leave her to it, though.

We'll come back to her.

Right now I want you to check *him* out.

In the front of the pack, a fit guy with a neatly-trimmed beard is setting the pace in an outfit that seems like maybe it was tailored for him. He looks backwards a few times at the rest of the team. Concern is knitted across his face. "You okay?" he keeps asking. Everyone nods back, assuring him they're fine, but he's not convinced. He's especially worried about one of his teammates, so he runs in front of her and says "jump on."

"What?" she says.

"I'll carry you," he insists.

"I'm fine!"

So he throws her over his shoulder, a fireman's carry.

For good measure, he spots another tired-looking runner and throws him over the other shoulder. You know, for balance.

Amazingly, he keeps running. The others look on in shock.

"Jump on," he tells them. And he's completely serious.

Meet Trip, the Hero.

Lesson 5

Heroism can be a form of self-destruction (the Trip lesson).

SUMMARY: Trip represents the Hero archetype. He is incredibly selfless and oriented towards people, which prevents confrontation among the staff working for his campaign for governor. Unfortunately, he takes on much more of his staff's responsibilities than he has time for, which exhausts his energy (I'll illustrate this using the metaphor of a Wellness Mine—that's "mine" like where coal is extracted). To counter this, Trip does a personal audit of his values and priorities, and braces himself to ask for what he will need in order to sustain his energy. To help with this, I recommend that Heroes (and everyone else) try a stress management exercise called Body Alarm (page 104).

Within a month of his campaign for governor, Trip was pulling late Saturday nights at headquarters. He'd strategically furnished his office with a futon, which he'd sleep on so he could wake up early to finalize the schedules for his phone bank volunteers.

"It's easier to get work done when nobody's here. I have a few more things to get done after this, and then I really should get home."

While a few volunteers tinkered away at spreadsheets on the other side of the suite, Trip poured hot water from his electric kettle into a "Vote Trip" mug filled with instant coffee grounds. A clothes rack with at least a week's worth of wardrobe, a mini fridge, and a toiletry bag were strewn around his office.

Thanks to a lively (and viral) string of public appearances during his primary campaign, Trip narrowly avoided a run-off election, and was headed into a general that was not a sure thing. He was what you'd call a "change candidate." In fact, the unlikeliness of his victory was part of what drew him to throw his hat in the ring.

From middle school student government president to city council to mayor, Trip had won every election he ran in. Time and time again, people found Trip inspiring. He helped people to see where there were opportunities to improve their communities, and to see the potential in themselves to make change happen. Whether he was helping his high school drama club successfully petition for permission to produce The Laramie Project or supporting a dozen chefs as they opened a fully immigrant-owned food cart pod, Trip brought the best out of other people.

He was great to work with, too. Among the staffers and volunteers who worked on his campaign, Trip was famous for writing really great recommendation letters (himself, of course). His team always mattered to him, and it showed.

He'd worked with the same campaign manager for the last 15 years, a woman named Heidi—who had abruptly quit after Trip won the recent primary. She assured him that the reason she'd needed to step down wasn't about him, it was about her fear of being in the national spotlight, but Trip took her departure very personally.

His new campaign manager was a bigwig from Washington, D.C., who was, for all intents and purposes, a much safer bet for what was becoming a high-profile election. Still, Trip stayed fixated on Heidi. "If I'd been better at delegating, Heidi probably would have stuck around." "If my office looked like this when Heidi was here, she probably would have run for the hills much sooner." "I just have to make sure I don't scare the new campaign manager away, too."

As Trip tinkered away at his schedule, he was haunted by the specter of Heidi over his shoulder. It wasn't that he thought he needed her to win the election, but he felt as though her departure indicated that he had already failed at some much more important goal: earning the loyalty of his team.

It consumed him to the point that, as more and more text messages piled up on his personal phone from his husband (who was getting tired of sleeping alone in a King-sized bed), Trip was compelled to watch the day's volunteers assemble, searching the crowd for his volunteer coordinator, Vic. He dialed Vic on his campaign phone, mumbling, "where the heck is he?"

A minute later, Trip glided down the hallway and passed a pair of star-struck volunteers who whispered, "Ohmigod!" and "Play it cool!"

Trip was totally smooth about it. "Thanks for being here!"

But he wasn't really looking at them, he was observing Vic at the head of the conference room. Vic looked harried—trying to cue up a slide show and slip off his scarf and jacket at the same time.

Trip looked at his watch. 9:01am.

He sailed into the conference room, transforming as he entered. Even without making a flashy entrance, his presence seemed to trigger the beginning of the orientation.

"Howdy folks, I'm so glad you're all here! I'll get us started while Vic gets our slideshow up and running…"

In about five seconds, Trip had reframed his volunteer coordinator as more of a stagehand than a facilitator—and both of them looked relieved.

While Trip waxed poetic about the symbolic importance of volunteer-driven campaigns, Vic got the slideshow running and put away his jacket and scarf. Trip played off his audience really well. Every time one of the volunteers interjected with a comment or a joke, Trip wasn't thrown off, he was excited and bantered back. He improvised brilliantly, and seemed to thrive off of the group's enthusiasm.

So instead of keeping this impromptu introduction a brief cameo, he said, "All right, why don't I walk us through the slideshow?"

Vic was a little bit taken aback, but not exactly disappointed, "Go for it."

From there, Trip walked the volunteers through how to use their contact info database, call script, and the nuances of their call system—even how to locate the hard-to-find mute button.

Vic got to sit back and simply click to the next slide.

Meanwhile, Trip's personal phone, neglected in his office, collected more and more notifications of text messages from his husband.

You might be a Hero if...

- The people you live with have to remind you to take off your shoes and contact lenses when you're home, so that you don't leave again.

- You can become trapped by the belief that you do things more efficiently than anyone else, so you should just do them.

- You occasionally find it difficult to answer the question, "How are you?" authentically—and sometimes give a polite (but untrue) response.

- You've updated your LinkedIn profile during a family vacation... twice.

- One of your bad habits is creating very difficult-to-achieve key performing indicators.

- You have a trophy shelf.

- You introduce yourself with your job title first and name second.

- You've practiced your "humble" acceptance speech in the mirror.

- You can't watch a show without Googling the actors' net worth.

- You've been known to run a 5K, just for the Instagram post.

- Your self-worth is inversely proportional to your email inbox count.

- You've joined a gym at least partially because of a networking opportunity.

The risks of completionism

Knowing how people like Trip work helps us understand how to help them succeed in their goals and share their gifts with the world—in a way that doesn't leave them totally fracked.

One of my nephews, who is really into video games, taught me the term "completionist." When a completionist plays Super Mario Bros., he doesn't just run through the levels and rescue Princess Peach as quickly as possible. Instead, he finds every coin in every level, unlocks all the secret worlds, and then replays the whole game in Hard Mode.

That's one way of thinking about Heroes, and it's easy to see the useful applications. In Trip's case, his completionism was a very helpful quality when he set a bunch of weight loss goals 15 years ago. He found a trainer (the one with the best reviews of anyone in the city), and reached his target weight in record time. He stayed on with Andy because they got along, and because he also offered a weight training program that Trip loves. "I used to be so out of shape I couldn't run a mile. I've done three marathons in the last two years, and I can bench 1-and-a-half-times my own weight."

But it was this completionism, and Trip's fear of imposing too much on his team, that put him on track to run balls-out. He'd started trying to rescue any aspect of his campaign that wasn't going perfectly, seemingly ready to do the work of anyone who worked on it. He was also alienating his husband, and would undoubtedly wake up one morning as a bachelor, with ulcers and/or high blood pressure, so exhausted from single-handedly winning his election that he'd be completely unable to govern.

Heroes like Trip often do something that I call "mining their own wellness."

Picture, beneath Trip's proud chest, his enormous heart. Inside his heart, there is a cave with a wooden placard that reads, "Wellness Mine: help yourself!"

And at all hours, day and night, Trip is constantly inviting others in. Swarm after swarm of swarthy people regularly march into the mine with pickaxes and hard hats in hand, ready to lay down tracks and send carts in and out of the depths to extract every last bit of his Wellness.

"You're sure we can take as much as we want?"

"Absolutely!" Trip boasts, "This stuff never runs out!"

He sends his own people into the Wellness Mine, too. "I've got a lot of people I'm trying to help, so bring me back as much material as you can. They're gonna need it!"

Down they go, prying Wellness off of the walls of Trip's heart, with his blessing. With each swing of the axe, he winces a little, but he never asks them to stop.

With or without meaning to, those on his team gobble up Trip's Wellness, too. He gives out freshly-mined Wellness for free to people like Vic, the new campaign manager, and his husband—all of whom would never presume to go into the cave themselves. None of them is capable of bringing themselves to swing an axe at Trip's heart.

That's because they know something Trip chooses to ignore: there is a finite amount of valuable material in the Wellness Mine. Painstakingly, the people who *will* take advantage of Trip (including Trip himself) plunder all the usable material until there's nothing left to take. Then, they seal up the entrance and leave it for the bats and gremlins to take over (or whatever happens to abandoned mines).

When you "mine" your own wellness, you're basically fracking yourself. The sad irony about people who mine their own wellness is that, even though they sacrifice their energy because they want to be useful and helpful, they wind up rendering themselves useless and helpless. Which ultimately creates problems for the very people they sacrificed for.

Point in case: the new campaign manager, brought up that she was concerned about Trip's schedule. Trip assured her she shouldn't worry. Next, Vic shared his worries about finding coverage for some of the campaign's weeknight events. Trip said he'd take care of it. Then, his husband brought up that he was concerned, too. Trip calmed him down with a kiss (and told him not to wait up tonight).

Trip let all of those warnings slide off his back.

But then his trainer Andy brought up that he might not be able to accommodate Trip's erratic schedule, "I don't mind switching up our regular meeting time, but I've got other clients to see, so I can't be meeting you at different times every week."

Why was it only Andy's warning that got through to Trip?

Trip is reliant on his fitness routine (which Andy gives him access to) in order to maintain a steady supply of Wellness. Without Andy, Trip is forced to confront the finiteness of his own energy reserves. It's as though he tried to deploy a miner, who scratched his head and said, "Into the Wellness Mine? Sorry dude, last time I went in there, that place was running out of good stuff *fast*."

Once Andy demonstrated that he was prepared to withdraw from this cycle of fracking, Trip was forced to reckon with the fact that his energy reserves were finite; his priorities were actually under threat.

Fortunately, unlike most mines, there are ways that Trip's Wellness Mine can be replenished. He took a moment to remind himself of the several ways he knew how, and wrote them down:

- Earn voters' trust.

- Delegate more tasks.

- Prioritize sleep.

- Build trust within my team.

- Have at least a little bit of an outside life.

- Tend to and strengthen my marriage.

A not-unreasonable list.

But as Trip compared this list to his calendar, he saw an enormous amount of asymmetry. He'd spent copious hours earning voters' trust and (in his way) building trust within his team. But how many hours had he actually spent nurturing his marriage? What was left of his "outside life"? Was crashing on a functional futon really a way to "prioritize" sleep? None of this sat well with him.

He'd told himself that this particular life "mode" was only temporary. Just for getting through the campaign. But as the limitations of his energy source began revealing themselves, he realized that, best case scenario, he'd become a governor. And then his schedule would become even *harder* to control.

So he pulled up his calendar with the goal of, at minimum, fitting in more time with his husband. He scrolled and clicked around for at least a full minute, sifting his way through settings, filters, and eventually two other calendars.

It was a complete mess.

He paused and reflected for a moment, and reminded himself that he'd spent his whole life facing impossible-seeming tasks—and won. After all, he'd gone from dropping a 30-pound barbell on his foot to lifting one-and-a-half times his own weight.

The world needs you, Hero, because:

- You are exceptionally good at seeing patterns and making connections.

- You inspire excellence in everyone around you.

- You bring vision to life, transforming ideas into actionable plans and tangible outcomes.

- You lead by example with your hard work and ambition.

- You show grace and efficiency in high-stakes situations.

- You bring energy and enthusiasm, infusing projects with momentum and a can-do spirit.

- You embody perseverance, showing that setbacks are just stepping stones to success.

- You encourage self-improvement, challenging yourself and others to continuously grow and evolve.

- You make dreams feel possible, bridging the gap between aspiration and achievement.

Points and boundaries

Trip's relationship with his trainer Andy was so nourishing and energizing because he guided Trip through a program of measurable tasks and habits. Want to become stronger? Master these lifting techniques. Next week, you'll be able to add weight. Next month, you'll be able to increase that weight by 5 pounds. And so on. Want to run a marathon? Let's focus on your gait. Next week, we'll see how far you can go. Next month, we'll start adding distance.

Trip, like many Heroes, loves points. He loves watching numbers go up. He doesn't love to triumph *over* people, but he certainly loves to *win*. Especially if he can win *with* people.

So, when I began working with Trip, we decided that a gamified approach would help enormously when it came to wresting control of his schedule, too.

He identified the amount of time he would need with his husband, per week, in order for him to feel that he was honoring his commitment to him (and to derive energy from the power source of his marriage). Then, he pinpointed how many hours per week of planned *and unplanned* public appearances were necessary for him to feel that he was adequately showing up for voters (a helpful way to identify a maximum capacity that was firm, but made space for improvisation). Perhaps most importantly, he identified who on his team had room in their schedules to take on additional responsibilities.

He stared at the new schedule, filled with big, clean blocks of color—instead of a maze of ifs, thens, conditions, and alternatives. Like a shiny present to himself. But he was thinking about his team. He was afraid of imposing on them. Of seeming weak. Of needing to ask for help.

As he caught himself twisting his wedding band (one of his nervous tics), he reminded himself that this process was *always* going to be difficult, but that it was also worth doing. He had to carry on for his husband, who he loved dearly. For his team, who he had so much faith in. For his voters, who he wanted to do right by. The discomfort was worth it.

The only way to honor his own ambition was to face that discomfort head on.

So, he grabbed a paper sign that he'd created for moments like this, stuck it on the door, swept out of the office, and began towards the door to the stairwell.

One of the staffers glanced up, familiar with this routine. "Have fun!" she offered through a smirk.

"Don't let anyone call an ambulance!" Trip replied through a bashful smirk.

The sign on Trip's door? It read, "Went for a scream in the stairwell. Back in 10."

Try This: Body Alarm

On some level, we write the rules for our boundaries in our pre-teen years. So when we get to adulthood, it's like owning an iPhone: we have to upgrade them constantly.

You're able to sniff out when, say, your family is going to ask us that same invasive question. Or when the all-hands meeting is gonna start going south. Or when the neighbor on the elevator is going to turn a situation into a political soapbox.

It's a safety mechanism we created for ourselves at a younger, tenderer age, when we first learned how to protect ourselves.

But sometimes our anticipation of distressing patterns is the thing that manifests them. What really happens is that, when you perceive that "turn," it's actually *you* who turns the meeting (or the family dinner or the elevator ride). At a minimum, you turn your danger lenses on, and now all you see is danger.

However, if you can upgrade your boundary and reinforce its permeability, give yourself more space, and activate your curiosity, you will have a totally different set of lenses on the same cyclical behavior!

There's always at least one person at work who's a total jerk, right?

Well, you're never going to get away from that guy, but the Body Alarm allows you to change who you are in that situation. Yep, you can do that today—by finding a place to go shout.

The trick is to use your responses to predictable, familiar threats (conspiracy theorist neighbor on the elevator) as a training ground for unpredictable, new challenges (stubborn crow hanging out in the conference room).

- Use it when you're ready to be treated differently.

- Use it when you're ready to get really different results from a repetitive scenario.

- Use it when you're ready to just feel better.

- Use it when taking a gentle, slow stroll isn't the right thing to regulate yourself.

- Use it to shift your body to a new normal.

- Use it when you realize that it's time to upgrade your threat-response instructions from middle school.

Body Alarm is a lot easier to focus on when someone is on-hand to walk you through it (especially the first time), but I'm sharing step-by-step instructions so you can at least identify some of the "variables" that fit in. If you'd rather watch a demonstration of these instructions go to book.vialucent.com.

1. **Choose an ick.** In order to find your Body Alarm, we do need to get into a kind of gross memory. I promise you, we're not going to stay there very long. This will usually be related to your current high-stakes situation. See if you can find a memory or a recurring issue that you'll have a chance to face again. Some ongoing situation in which you hope to be treated differently or you would appreciate very different results. Something you'd just really like to feel better about afterward.

   Experience that memory until you get to the point when you knew things were about to go bad. *That* is usually the moment the Body Alarm shows up.

2. **Notice what part of your body activates.** Close your eyes and do a body scan. There is a part of your body that just woke up. It's letting you know it's there— where is it? What does it feel like? Is it an object? A feeling? Does it have a texture? Is it a flavor or a thing? Is it a color? For me, it's like an arrow, lodged in my throat.

3. **Shake it off.** Open your eyes and shake your arms out. Try to say your phone number backwards. Bring yourself back to the present moment.

4. **Notice the edge.** Next, we're going to expel that unpleasant feeling. For me, it looks like pulling that arrow out of my throat. Give yourself enough room to take one step forward. Trip was able to do this on the landing between floors 2 and 3.

   Next, imagine that feeling. Put your arms out in front of you, and don't quite lock your elbows. Imagine that the triggering situation is on the other side of your palms. The space from the back of your hands to you is your boundary, your space. I want you to slowly bring that situation towards your body until your ick lights up.

   Okay, you found the safe distance between you and this trigger. Any closer, and you'd feel panic. Any further, and the sensation might go away.

5. **Evict the ick.** Think about how you're going to remove that unpleasant feeling from the part of your body that you identified. I recommend using two hands (I'm going to grab the arrow in my throat and pull it out).

And as you do this, you're going to shout.

Very loudly.

Yeah, we're gonna scream real loud. I do this all the time, and nobody has talked to me about it. Either they don't mind, or they don't hear it.

I like the word "no" or the F word, but I want you to pick a sound or a word that helps *you* have a better boundary, that helps *you* have more space.

Get ready by taking a slow, intentional breath. Know that you're going to get the whole thing.

Count backwards from three, and evict the ick as you shout.

1. **Repeat.** Think, "I know that this works. I trust it." Take a big, slow breath, and repeat step five.

2. **Create more space.** Now, put your hands up to where your boundary was, and exhale. Push it out in front of you. Out to the sides. Above you. Even behind you.

3. You are pushing that situation farther away from you. I want you to really *feel* the space that you're creating, how real it is. It's important to do this part slowly and thoughtfully.

   What you're telling your body right now is that you have so much more space.

4. You have so much more time.

5. That you're really well protected.

6. **Upgrade your operating system.** Now, go back to that situation you've been holding in mind.

You may be aware of something that you weren't aware of before. You may feel differently. You may be able to access *curiosity*. How could you show up differently if that situation repeats itself? You could get pissed and confront it directly. You could stop putting yourself in the position to experience it over and over again. You could put in the energy to try to interrupt the pattern and ask for something else. The possibilities are vast.

7. Cross your arms in front of you and use your hands to tap your own arms really, *really*, **really** slowly. Left, right, left, right, left, right.

8. Doing this helps you to integrate your new skill. The next time you revisit the scenario that caused the Body Alarm to go off, you will experience it in a new way. Tapping helps your new response become more real than your automatic response.

Why this works

When we feel threatened and our Body Alarm is going off, our curiosity is offline. You can't be in curiosity mode and in danger mode at the same time; it's a light switch. What we focus on determines what we miss. The Body Alarm exercise allows you to shift your focus away from your fear and toward your curiosity.

This works even if you're artificially asking yourself an open-ended question, like "What might it be like to show up differently here?"

The Body Alarm exercise gives you more space, so that new situations feel like less of an attack or less dangerous.

Let's use my arrow-in-the-throat example: if it feels like an arrow is coming at me and I have X amount of space, that's not enough time to do anything. When I upgrade my boundary, I give myself more space. I can't control whether or not new arrows will come at me (they will), and I can't control what everyone else will do in that situation. But I *can* turn that arrow into a little aimless white butterfly. I *can* give myself time to be like, "What are you doing in here?"

Being curious about a butterfly is a much healthier place to respond from than being terrified of an arrow.

(For Harry Potter fans: it's like shouting Riddikulus at a boggart.)[5] [6]

---

[5] While this book includes exercises you might also find in therapy or self-help spaces, this is not a therapeutic manual, nor am I a therapist.

[6] The author of this book does not support the transphobic behavior of the author of the Harry Potter series.

Segue

We're back on the running track.

Trip has somehow finagled four runners into his grip, and, while the sheer mechanics are impressive, our pace has slowed in a big way. Trip is weighed down, dragged lower and lower. He's spending all of his energy just trying to remain upright and keep going. It's less like he's running and more like he's falling forwards but managing to stay upright. If he keeps doing this, he's going to face-plant. We all will. Mouthfuls of gravel, bodies crushing together. And as we try to pick ourselves up, we'll stumble blindly down the slope, dragging each other into the Petri Dish of Burnout.

But that's not happening, because Trip is about to make a different choice.

Let's leave him to it, though.

We'll come back to him.

For now, I want you to check out that lady. She's toward the back of the pack, but keeping pace, the sturdy woman with curly dark hair wearing all those cool gadgets. Her running outfit is average but practical. Her eyes dart from the track to the rope to the smartwatch to the runners to the smartwatch to the track to the smartwatch to the runners.

Then, she starts asking the other runners how they're feeling.

"What's your heart rate like?"

"What'd you have for dinner last night?"

"Why are you pinching your side? Do you have a cramp?"

They're a little taken aback, but they try and answer her questions to put her at ease.

"When was the last time you had water?"

"How are you feeling?"

"Hey, put on this heart monitor, I wanna keep an eye on your vitals."

Now, she's passing around heart monitors and connecting them all to her Bluetooth dashboard. Everyone is praying that this will satisfy her enough to leave them alone. Instead, after crunching the numbers, she reaches a conclusion: the group should sprint up the next hill.

"The data say we can do it."

Needless to say, this earns her a lot of side-eye.

Meet Fiona, the Researcher.

Lesson 6

Researching can be a form of delaying (the Fiona lesson).

SUMMARY: Fiona represents the Researcher archetype. She is hyperlogical and thorough, which helps her navigate the many technical questions and challenges that come with her work recycling parts of windmills. However, she is distractible, and commits her attention to projects that are not the best use of her talents (which I illustrate with the metaphor of a Never-Ending Existential Research Project™). To counter this, Fiona creates a logical method for identifying more productive and energizing uses of her time. To help with this, I recommend that Researchers (and everyone else) try an intention-setting mantra practice called Lover Words (page 129).

Fiona was very careful when she chose me out of the million-and-a-half "coaches" that came up on her Google search. She told me that I met all the criteria on her spreadsheet, plus I was local to her, plus my website referred specifically to working with folks in climate. Fiona was the Chief Technology Officer (and employee number three) at a startup that was looking to streamline the recycling process for windmills.

"I need some strategies for getting everyone aligned. I explain things super clearly, but then everyone shoots holes in it, or they act like they don't understand—and when things don't come together it makes me look bad. I think I just need a more methodical approach, and I'm hoping you can teach me the best one for my situation."

She even assessed me with a rubric during our discovery call, glancing back and forth between our Zoom call and a second monitor.

"What kinds of frameworks do you use?" "Do you give your clients toolkits?" "Can you send me any case studies or testimonials from your former clients talking about what their outcomes were like?" "How long have you been coaching, by the way?" "Do all of your clients work in climate?" "Or is that a newer niche for you?"

A week later, we met on the patio of a coffee shop that was equidistant between our offices. She was warm and polite when she greeted me, but a little out of breath and carrying a pair of paper shopping bags overflowing with books from Moon Palace (a great indie bookstore in Minneapolis).

"Required reading, according to six different anti-racist book lists."

It was fall 2020; those book lists were making the rounds, and Fiona was responsible for writing a DEI statement on behalf of her company. More accurately: she'd volunteered to write it. The C-suite was eager to put something out there before more of their peers in the industry beat them to it.

"Writing this letter is a microcosm of my job. It has the DNA of everything I'm trying to deal with right now: my responsibilities as a leader of this team, my issues with time management, my struggles with getting the team to congeal around anything, my duties as a person with white privilege. Plus: if I can get this right, everyone will stop doubting me about everything else."

Fiona wanted a surefire method of identifying and executing an objectively "correct" way of writing this statement. This was how she chased every responsibility, with a pair of tweezers, trying to contour everything she did into some imagined "perfection."

She knew that writing this statement wouldn't solve all of her problems at work, but saw it as an opportunity to learn a new way to be in a more sustainable relationship with her work and with her team. She'd also assigned an immense amount of importance to the letter. It didn't matter to her that her team had actually offered to take the letter off her plate. In fact, that only motivated her to prove herself even more.

"I already told them I'd take care of it, so I'm gonna take care of it and write one that'll be better than Corey's. I told them that I just need time to do it the right way. This is what I mean: no one trusts me. But they will when they read my version of the statement."

You might be a Researcher if...

- You frequently volunteer to manage challenges that no one else seems to understand or perceive. When you report back, it takes ten minutes to explain everything you've done, and eventually the people on your team say, "cool, yeah, great, thanks for doing that," just to shut you up and move on.

- You pack more books than clothes when going on vacation.

- You've ever Googled "how to avoid small talk at parties."

- You prefer to think things through carefully before taking action.

- People describe you as emotionally distant or detached, but you know it's because you're more drawn to intellectual conversations than talking about everyone's feelings.

- You get excited about new information and perspectives the way others get excited about puppies.

- Your YouTube history looks like a PhD syllabus.

- You avoid phone calls by sending a detailed email instead.

- You've calculated your exact amount of social interaction needed before recharging.

- You've been called a "walking encyclopedia" more times than you can count—but you counted anyway.

- You've built an Excel sheet to track your favorite fictional universes.

- Your dream job involves minimal human interaction and unlimited internet access.

- You've fact-checked a movie while still watching it.

Never-Ending Existential Research Projects™

The DEI statement proved to only be a tipping point in an ongoing struggle.

Fiona's research into energy-efficient software led the company to move email platforms six times in the last five years. And it wasn't always about the work itself, either. A stray suggestion that the company send out sustainable goody bags turned into a three-month side quest (but also a really frickin' awesome-sounding goody bag that could win awards).

Fiona was in the habit of turning work projects into what you might call Never-Ending Existential Research Projects™.

A Never-Ending Existential Research Project™ is what happens when an organized and thorough person tries to complete a task that is disorganized and poorly-defined. It's when the numerator is infinity and the denominator is zero. A never-ending amount of material tries to fill a container with no bottom.

It's a scream—no, a pointlessly thorough lecture—delivered into a void.

Picture Fiona standing at a lectern at the edge of a cliff. She is shuffling her papers, double-checking the facts on her pitch deck, quickly adding in another section. She apologizes to her audience at the bottom of the canyon: a smattering of cactuses, tumbleweeds, and thirsty lizards.

Now, the *quality* of Fiona's presentation of her findings from this Never-Ending Existential Research Project™ is top-notch. There's no doubt about that.

But the preparation never ends. The presentation never reaches a conclusion. It only echoes a few times before it fades.

Fiona's hyperfixation on the DEI statement created a particularly high-stakes knot of missed deadlines, interpersonal conflict, and philosophical spiraling—to the point that her well-meaning colleagues noticed that she was being detrimental to herself. So they did something that they hoped would be for Fiona's own good:

They placed her on a 2-week mandatory leave.

Fiona was surprised when the call came from HR, but she felt some reassurance when her "work bestie" sent her an email from his personal account. "Everyone wants you to come back as soon as possible. We all agree that you're the hardest worker. You've prevented every single one of us from missing some important element in our work. But you need to rest, for your sake."

Fiona knew exactly what he meant, but she was still upset. "It's the first time they've done this to anyone in the company, and they did it to *me*, which is pretty intense because *I* was the one who *hired* them." Still, she took this as an opportunity to regroup. "I want to be able to come back and demonstrate to them that I'm ready, that I've learned, that I've done the soul-searching I needed to and that I know how to get right back into action."

But, she realized, she couldn't treat this redemption journey as yet another Never-Ending Existential Research Project™ with the same driving-yourself-crazy attitude that had exhausted her resources in the first place.

It was difficult for Fiona, because Researchers don't abandon their projects. Heck no. They're not slowing down, and they'll bulldoze anyone who tries to make them do unnecessary busywork.

It's easy to see how much power there is in Fiona's busy mind and thorough habits. It's also easy to see how Researchers can easily waste their power.

Wasted energy. Windmills. Unnecessary battles against artificial foes. Sound familiar?

The word quixotic refers to the eponymous Don Quixote, who famously rides into battle with windmills, thinking they are threatening giants. He's so distracted by his own theories that he winds up getting tangled in the sail of one of the windmills, knocking him off his horse. He's so attached to his version of reality that he insists that his antagonist *was* a giant—transfigured to *look* like a windmill by a magician.

Now, I see a couple of lessons in *Don Quixote* for Fiona. The obvious one is that, like Don Quixote, she needlessly spent energy in her battles with manufactured challenges. But less talked about is the flip side; she also got herself beat the heck up by an inanimate object that never would have hurt her if she hadn't charged at it so, well, quixotically.

Are you charging at windmills?

I get it; you want your team to see what you see. You want them to know what you know, that there *are* giants out there among the windmills.

The trick is to make sure that the foes you set out to vanquish are the right ones. In Fiona's case, the big baddie wasn't a DEI statement—it was the very premise of a Never-Ending Existential Research Project™.

The numbers don't lie

Fiona sat down to take an inventory of the time she spent on each of her projects over the last month. She even logged the editing history of all the spreadsheets she'd worked on to see how long she spent tinkering on each of them.

Which was heaven for her. She entered a kind of flow state, copying and pasting and formulating an impressively thorough spreadsheet, which revealed to her that she had worked an average of 64.6 hours a week.

She began to justify this to herself. "Well, when you're C-suite for a startup, you can't really hold yourself to a job description. It's not like when I was in my carefree 20s, when I had time to do things like teach dance classes three times a week." But she sat with the fact that she had calculated a 64.6-hour work week and felt that there was nothing she could do about it. She realized this data could tell a more complex story.

With a bit more tinkering, Fiona sorted out her data and itemized them into color-coded category types. About 25% of the rows were blue, for "explicitly in my job description," about 25% of them were red, for "not in my job description," and the remaining 50% were purple, for "arguably my job."

Then, she evaluated each of her individual tasks, giving them a "score" (on a scale of 1-10), that corresponded to that task's degree of positive impact on the company. This was hard for her to do, in part because such a score is subjective, and in part because many of the tasks were taken on in order to prevent setbacks or maintain a status quo.

Still, the data told a sobering story. Fiona was spending way too much time trying to perfectly execute tasks that a) weren't her responsibility, b) didn't require her actual skill set, and c) didn't contribute to the company's growth.

Instead of trying to convince herself to take things *off* her plate, she did the opposite, brainstorming more things to pile *onto* that plate.

She retreated into her mind for a moment, "Well, we really should be applying for grants…" And then the glimmer appeared in her eyes. She took a deep breath and dove in. "There are conferences I want to go to. There are podcasts that people on our team need to be on. There are plans to hire an ops team that we've kept on the back burner for *years*…" She kept going. Getting detailed. Getting energized. Getting nerdy. Getting *giddy*.

The world needs you, Researcher, because:

- We need your mind, your ideas, your leadership, your thoroughness, your creativity. We need your fascination with challenges that haven't been solved yet.

- You turn complex problems into understandable solutions.

- You are constantly seeing what others miss.

- You help the rest of us see the world through a well-informed lens.

- You value independence, showing how self-reliance can lead to innovative thinking.

- You offer calm and composure, bringing steadiness in moments of uncertainty or chaos.

- You are a great listener, absorbing information before speaking, which makes your contributions profound and valuable.

- You ensure that things are never attempted without being thoughtfully examined first.

- You see connections others might miss, linking ideas and concepts in new and insightful ways.

- You remind us that knowledge is power, and that learning is a lifelong journey.

There is no book

Researchers like Fiona want to be the ones to find the answers. Nothing turns them on more than being told, "no one's figured it out yet."

And it's that quality that makes them both so suited for work in climate *and* so vulnerable to it. They look for perfect answers. They don't want seams or loose ends or a margin of error. They expect that there's a "right answer." If it were a math problem, you could find the solution in the back of the book. But with the problems of climate change, there is no solution in the back of the book. There is no book.

When Researchers are well, they can pull things together that no one else can. But when Researchers feel that nobody understands them, that they're only being tolerated, they slip into a Never-Ending Existential Research Project™ that leaves them exhausted and wastes their gift. When they feel that their observations are being challenged, they do hours of data collection and presentation to re-assert their authority, thinking that is the best use of their gifts. In Fiona's case, she slips into survival mode, and compensates for her difficult feelings by doing all that red stuff on her spreadsheet.

Fiona's amazing capacity for research and detail wasn't needed in the realm of about 70% of the responsibilities she convinced herself to take on, like being on the hiring committee for a department she's not in. It isn't that she wasn't doing a good job in those areas—in fact, I'm sure she was nailing all of it. It's that those things can be managed by someone else who could do the same thing 85% as well as she could, but with a much smaller fraction of energy.

That would free Fiona up to direct her attention toward the kinds of things no one else can do. The kinds of things no one has done before. The kinds of things that made her basically salivate.

On the day before she was due to return to work, Fiona was back at the coffee shop with her laptop and folders and notebooks with all her color-coded post-its. She had begun her offensive against her biggest foe yet: the very premise of a Never-Ending Existential Research Project™ itself.

She had identified all the outer layer items that she could peel off of her schedule to make space for the things she was actually excited about—and *was the right person for.* Not only had she picked a bunch of things to take off of her schedule, she had sent the necessary emails and received the necessary permissions from her teammates to actually do so. She stepped down from the search committee. She let Corey publish his DEI statement. She bowed out of recurring meetings she didn't need to be at. She even relinquished her oversight of the team's day-to-day operations functions to the COO.

"Oh! Our meeting's going to fall apart without you!" said one of the ops coordinators. "Things are gonna start slipping through the cracks."

Fiona was sad as well. The work tasks she was walking away from all felt important, worthwhile, and necessary—and made her feel important, worthwhile, and necessary, too.

But she had looked at the data, and the only way for her to have a healthy relationship to work was to carve out a workload that was realistically only 40 hours per week. Anything more would degrade the quality of her work. Intellectually, she understood this, but her body wanted to reject it.

She had another challenge, too: a gigantic, abstract to-do list and a ton of gaps on her calendar.

"Whoa," she said, "I haven't had this much unstructured time since... right after college."

Back then, she had a part-time job as a kind of underling for her professor, which gave her the flexibility to follow her bliss. She volunteered with a climate advocacy group a few nights a month. She was in a book club. She lived in her mother's house to save money and helped with her garden. She picked up contracts when something interested her. And she went to a dance studio to teach and choreograph on weekends.

"I was just having fun—my life was so *flexible*. I really could have jumped right into a full-time job. But you know what…" she seemed to fade away for a second, but then she came back. "I was *very* productive in that part-time job. I wrote a *ton* of software. Some of it I still use!" Then she smiled. "Maybe this new schedule won't be the end of the world."

And so Fiona went into work the next day, resolved. She had accepted the fact that she was able to do more when she had less on her plate to think about.

She cruised right along with that energy for about a week, before facing the dilemma so many do after getting exactly what they say they want.

The honeymoon ends

One of the new priorities Fiona was most excited to focus her reclaimed energy on was weighing in about the company's marketing strategy, specifically to share her insights about how they could make a big splash using a few smart podcast appearances. Fiona was a big fan of podcasts about renewable energy. One summer, while on a family vacation, her parents had to beg her to stop subjecting everyone to hours of My Climate Journey's *Inevitable* podcast while she cooked, and just put on some jazz.

So it was with great enthusiasm that she joined the marketing team. They were happy to welcome Fiona in; everyone knew how knowledgeable she was.

"It's an open secret that Fiona's the go-to person when the marketing team needs someone with a science brain to fact-check our language," said one of the copywriters. "She goes above and beyond. Not only does she make connections between ideas that I hadn't made before, but she's corrected *my* punctuation usage."

At Fiona's first meeting with the team, the director of marketing walked her through the existing projects and plans.

"And how about podcasts?" Fiona asked.

"Oh, I wish!" laughed the director. "We're not ready for those yet!" Then she moved on with her spiel about SEO articles.

Fiona was mildly horrified, and did not have a good time at the full marketing team meetings, either. She watched them all plod along with a plan that, in her opinion, was uninspiring, conservative, generic, and arbitrary. As she looked at the other boxes on the Zoom call, she compared herself with the others on the team. Fiona had the longest tenure in the company, she was the highest ranked, she was the only one with a degree in engineering, and she was the only one who had even *heard* of *A Matter of Degrees*.

They need to trust me on this, Fiona screamed quietly behind her eyeballs. *Getting on those podcasts would blow us out of the water in a way that advertising a webinar on our pathetic little newsletter never will.*

But it was her first meeting, and the appropriate thing to do was observe quietly.

Less appropriate: she asked the marketing director for a sidebar later that day.

"I totally get why you want us to be on podcasts," they told her, "but it's too soon. Even if we blow up in popularity, we don't have strong enough content or products or services to direct them to, and that makes us look bad. That's what we need to shore up first before we ask for too much visibility beyond our circle of trust."

Fiona nodded. She understood. There was a dimension about this idea that she hadn't considered and wasn't paying attention to.

But still.

There must be other podcasts that would be more right-sized, that would be a good place for the team to develop their messages, or at least put them in front of some potential funders, that way they could give themselves some more *runway*.

It wasn't long before Fiona was rearing back, ready to sprint after one more Never-Ending Existential Research Project™. She was tapping a microphone, sending loud echoes down an uninterested valley. She was scribbling notes onto a towering pile of index cards. She was preparing yet another spreadsheet for an eternal grid of empty folding chairs.

In reality, she was sitting at her dining table at 10:00 p.m., scrounging the internet for even more climate-related podcasts instead of putting away her half-eaten dinner.

Fiona caught herself. She was acting totally out of balance, and she had missed some important aspects of the marketing strategy when she became fixated on the idea of podcast appearances. She realized that she was primarily protecting her ego by trying to prove that her first impulse was a viable idea, rather than accepting that marketing was *not her responsibility*, and that she didn't need to figure out what role podcasts should play for their company, if any.

So, she shut her computer.

She shook off some icky feelings.

And she opened her notebook.

Try this: Lover Words

We have a long driveway at our house in Saint Paul, and we share quite a lot of that driveway with our neighbor. The property line is right down the middle of it, and when shoveling the driveway, I absolutely can slip into autopilot because I *love* doing outdoor chores.

That's me. I'm the one who will come and untangle everybody's extension cord, and I'll do my best not to judge you for *letting* them get tangled.

Anyway, I often get into the driveway and enter autopilot. My autopilot is to literally put my head down and just plow through it, and I can get through hours of chores that way.

But I've become able to pause and notice that I'm sweating and breathing hard. Able to stand up and stretch my back out and to look around and notice how beautiful the morning snow is. Able to make choices that are right for me and, most importantly, to conserve my energy for what matters most instead of spending it all unconsciously.

Anytime you catch yourself in autopilot, you're no longer in autopilot. Any pause, any awareness.

Start where you are. Do what you can. Allow it to be a practice.

A wonderfully anchoring way of beginning that work is with Lover Words.

What do I mean about Lover Words? To begin, I'm going to talk about an archetype. This is not a human, this is an idea: the lover.

The lover archetype looks at a transactional opportunity and thinks, *I know who I am. I know how I want to feel. I know what I want. And I will have that, or I'll have nothing.* The lover's a badass.

The inverse to lover energy is to go through the world motivated to have successful transactions. The lover's opposite approaches transactions thinking, *I will meet the conditions I need to meet. I will be who you need me to be. I will show up as the person who makes a successful transaction.*

At some level, all ambitious people have been taught to have that mentality of centering the transaction without meaningfully considering themselves. *I will mold myself into who I need to be so that the deal happens.* In a lot of ways, our education system is set up like this. "The factory-mind-set school system is a relic of the industrial age, designed to produce workers for factories—workers who are trained to comply, fit in, and fear standing out."[7]

The good news is that you have an incredible ability to shift what you see, what you are aware of, what you have access to—so long as you can catch when you're thinking, *I will be who I need to be, so that the transaction happens.* Doing that gives you access to new realms of data that you weren't noticing before. You begin to notice new aspects of your experience, like what is happening to your energy, what you like and dislike, and what does and doesn't serve you.

You can reclaim your story and move closer to embodying the lover archetype by talking about and identifying your Lover Words. You have the sovereign right to declare how you want to feel and use that decision as a filter to see if an experience is for you or if it is not for you.

Hold up, you might be thinking. *I'm sorry, would you repeat that?*

Yep. Hardly anyone believes me the first time I say this.

You can decide how you want to feel.

---

[7] Godin, Seth. *Linchpin: Are You Indispensable?* New York: Portfolio, 2010.

Yes, you. *You* have the sovereign ability, as if you're DIYing your own wedding.

If it were a wedding, you'd decide how you want to feel, and use that decision as a filter. Is that the right thing for me on my wedding day, or is it not for me? Am I showing up in a way that allows me to cultivate those feelings in my body, or not?

I want you to choose between two and eight "feeling" words that you want to be present in the landscape of your life.

If it helps, go to feelingswheel.com, and check out the orange section for some inspiration. But you can pick whatever words you want.

Do you see a word that is winking at you?

That might be a place to consider starting. Then, use those words as a filter to look through, and help you decide whether something is for you—or not.

Dr. Joe Dispenza posits that "By the time we're 35 years old, 95 percent of who we are is a memorized set of behaviors, emotional reactions, unconscious habits, hardwired attitudes, beliefs, and perceptions that function like a computer program."[8] The way I see it, you automatically

---

[8] Dispenza, Joe. Breaking the Habit of Being Yourself: How to Lose Your Mind and Create a New One. Carlsbad, CA: Hay House, 2012.

process the data coming in through your five senses into autopilot thoughts, behaviors, and feelings.

We are walking machines of perception. Have you ever noticed that you can witness the same event as someone else, but walk away with completely different memories of what happened?

The Lover Words I unconsciously used to have were the result of my habits—part of the 95% that was automatic. We all have these. My old Lover Words probably sounded a lot more like "afraid," "aggressive," "frustrated." And when I had that filter, that's what I experienced until a wave of laws targeting transgender people started accelerating a couple of years ago. I started to have thoughts like, *I shouldn't fly. What if I'm flying from sanctuary state Minnesota to sanctuary state California, and I get rerouted to Oklahoma? I don't wanna be in an airport in Oklahoma. Maybe I should just stay home, y'all.* I'm someone who's filled up a passport and had to have pages sewed into it. I'm not a stay-at-home kind of person. But that started to be my reality.

I was proactively *not* booking flights because at some level my body started to associate travel with fear and danger. When I became aware of that pattern, I thought, *that's not who I am. I don't want that in my life.*

The power of the Lover Words lies in our ability to pick new ones and practice using them as a filter.

When I picked my current Lover Words (which are "safe," "whole," and "belong"), I literally started to see new things. I began to step out of things that I had been very engaged in or very attentive to. I allowed myself to wander into new things that I hadn't had the energy to pursue. I decided that I'm safe and I'm whole and I belong everywhere I go. And it was in cultivating the feeling of being safe, getting on an airplane no matter what was going to happen with rerouting, that I stopped letting those feelings control me. I still feel them, I just don't let them *drive*.

I don't have those frightened thoughts anymore because those experiences are not for me. Keeping my thumb on the pulse of all the laws that are getting passed, that's not for me. That doesn't support feeling safe, whole, and belonging. Now, to be sure, I'm *not* tuning out what's happening—I'm just not obsessively consuming.

Consider the words you choose constantly. Start using them as a filter. Which are the areas in your life you can change how you show up in? Can you stop engaging in it? Or just turn the valve way down on it so you don't have as much of it in your life? If you say it out loud, you're more likely to do it.

I solemnly swear to you, there are treasure chests full of goodness in exploring this in a way that feels accessible. That thing that you want will be easier to have when you feel safe getting it. It may feel like you're faking it, but the weirder it feels, the more you're doing it right.

Pick words that feel aspirational and accessible. You can also try them on for a little while and change them any time they stop feeling right.

Segue

We're back on the running track.

Fiona is so focused on knowing the details of everything that is happening around her that she fails to see the big picture. With her attention on everyone's vitals, winds up being surprised by a bump in the road. Rather than reacting to the shock of tripping on the bump, she gets distracted by figuring out where it came from. Unless she can pull herself away from giving all of her energy towards grasping our situation, she is going to keep us from responding *to it*. We'll miss seeing the forest for the trees. We'll also miss seeing the branches and the roots, which will get tangled up in our limbs, and *snap! Crunch! Pop!* Was that a stick breaking, or an ankle? Either way, we're a crackling, crumbling tumbleweed, rolling helplessly down into the Petri Dish of Burnout.

That's if Fiona keeps doing what she's doing.

But that's not happening, because the Lover Words in Fiona's book will help her make a different choice.

Let's leave her to it, though.

We'll come back to her.

I want you to check out one more guy, the toughest one in the group. He's comfortably situated in the middle over there. He is extremely casual, wearing a simple, ratty running outfit that he's been exercising in forever.

"Pick it up," he tells the runners behind him, "you can do it."

The leaders of the pack hear him and slow down a bit, to allow the others a chance to catch up.

"Don't slow down," he warns them, "we can all run faster than this."

He gives a few of his compatriots an encouraging pat on the back, but their eyes are full of alarm.

"You're bleeding," someone warns him.

"Eyes forward," he says, ignoring a widening gash along his heel, "we're gonna win this."

This is Eisen, the Motivator.

Lesson 7

Motivation can be a form of antagonizing (the Eisen lesson).

SUMMARY: Eisen represents the Motivator archetype. He is an ambitious CEO of an EV rental startup, where he has carved out an enormous opportunity while maintaining a crystal-clear vision that feels within reach. But the specificity and singularity of his vision is causing friction within the company culture, leading to a ton of turnover, including his co-founder (and best friend). He receives feedback that his management style feels like what I call the CPGI (which is a metaphor that I don't feel like giving away in the summary). In order to find a way forward, Eisen gets curious about his friend's experience in order to learn what he has missed. He is able to feel grounded when doing because he has practiced a visualization exercise that helps him regain a feeling of Gravitas (page 152).

It was pedal to the metal time, literally and figuratively.

Eisen was the CEO of a company that was poised to be the one to be the electric alternative to both the rideshare and rental car markets. Thanks to Eisen's long range vision, he'd started working on the concept more than 15 years ago, when Uber first entered the market. Since then, he'd worked out a lot of the kinks, questions, and complications while anticipating the "tipping point" moment of electric vehicle availability. Now that EVs were becoming all the rage, there were plenty of competitors out there, but they were new, naive, and reactive. Eisen's company was getting there first, and was better-prepared.

It was time to recruit a team of regional representatives to navigate the particular circumstances of each of their phase one markets, which were spread across North America and Europe.

"The energy is really incredible," he said while swaying back and forth onto his heels in the parking lot of their headquarters. In front of him was a row of EVs emblazoned with their branding. "I said I'd be really happy if we could earn enough funding to launch in at least six different cities," he said, smirking, "but I'm this close to getting us up to ten. I've proven we can handle it, I just have to show it in the budget."

It helps to have multiple guilty-feeling automobile corporations with desperate sustainability departments bidding for visibility.

"We just have to hire the right reps."

The company had what Eisen called a "retention issue." Namely: it had been hard to onboard and keep new talent.

Eisen and his best friend from college, Sally, had co-founded the company, but the director-level roles were a revolving door. Everyone working under those directors were vulnerable to the "weather patterns" above their heads. Some weathered the storms and stuck with it, but about half of them came and went with the people who hired them.

"Our value proposition isn't rocket science, but what's become clear to me is that not everyone comes here to do the work, if that makes any sense," Eisen said, clenching his jaw and slipping into a darker mood. "A lot of people think it's going to be an easy job: clock in, clock out, do what you're told. Not everyone has an interest in creating things, in figuring it out with us."

In other words: the work culture was scaring people away.

"When you're hiring people, it's hard to know who's just BSing you and who's serious when they say they're ready for that type of work. Some people just tell you what you want to hear in the interviews, and then six months later, they're out the door." He clenched his jaw even tighter. "So you wind up wasting all this time replacing them, losing momentum, sifting through all the unfinished stuff they left behind."

If Eisen took these losses personally, he wasn't showing it.

"I try my hardest to push people to see it as more than just a job, it's an opportunity to create the future of EV rentals. To see what we can do when we get to a niche market before anyone else. And if someone can't see that, you can't force them to. You have to move on and find someone who can."

This "retention issue" was the bugaboo of the company. As CEO, Eisen was forced to answer for the company's turnover to both Sally and the board. This had come to a head recently, after the HR director submitted a report on the subject, which revealed that the primary theme in exiting employees' complaints over the last three years was "company culture," the very thing that Eisen took so much pride in.

Now that they needed to hire people who would work very independently, and whose regional knowledge was indispensable, the company couldn't afford to not retain the ten reps.

Sally nodded to Eisen, agreeing that they "need to really invest in this problem," as though they had the same idea of what that meant. First, Eisen suggested that the company schedule a nature retreat to boost morale. Sally got really quiet. And then she suggested that Eisen hire someone to help him with his management style. The other folks on the executive team meeting looked at the floor to give Eisen a moment to digest. This was more than a suggestion from his co-founder, it was an ultimatum from his best friend.

"So that's what I've got to figure out," Eisen said. "How to create a work culture where people can get whatever they need in order to keep up."

While he cared deeply about the people he worked with and enjoyed spending time with them socially, he was not a person who spent much time thinking directly about the relational elements of work.

"I'd rather do work than talk about work," he said, often. "My philosophy is that that's how you learn how you work. Not books or classes."

You might be a Motivator if...

- You believe rules are guidelines—optional ones.

- You thrive on confrontation the way others thrive on caffeine.

- Your friends ask for your advice because they know you'll give it to them straight—whether they want it or not.

- You've turned a friendly game night into a full-on competition, with a prize.

- You've ever argued with a GPS because you know a better route.

- You lead meetings even when you're not the official leader.

- You've rearranged a room in someone else's home without them asking.

- You've ever declared, "Let's just get it done!" in a brainstorming session.

- People think you're strong, assertive, and unfeeling, but some part of you understands that this is because you struggle with vulnerability and expressing your emotions.

- Your negotiation tactics are legendary—and sometimes feared.

- You see obstacles as challenges and challenges as opportunities.

- You've considered a career in motivational speaking, whether the world's ready for it or not.

The pool noodle

Eisen attributed some of his challenges with junior colleagues to a difference in cultural work ethic; most of the new recruits were private and arts school graduates from California, used to being encouraged to follow their bliss. Eisen went to an all-boys Catholic school in Austria, and was used to structure, discipline, and hierarchy. He was a high school athlete, and briefly considered playing professional baseball, but stuck with business school instead because he saw more long term potential with his mind than with his body. Outside of work, he was an avid taekwondo student who was picking up escalating black belt degrees—not that he was a showoff.

Eisen and his wife had two sons, who he was very adorable with.

In one of his favorite videos, his son Felix is successfully riding his bicycle without handlebars for the first time. Behind him, Eisen follows with a folded up pool noodle, which he uses to gently nudge his son along.

"Catch me!" Felix keeps shouting. "Catch me! Catch me!"

"You're not falling!" Eisen tells him, through infections giggles. "Keep going, keep going!"

"I'm not falling!" Felix realizes aloud. "I'm *going*!"

It's one of those videos that really should go viral.

The pool noodle is one version of what I'll call a CPGI, I'll tell you what that stands for later, but just know this: a CPGI is something that Motivators like Eisen use in order to keep people moving, to help them reach their potential, and to provide negative feedback. In this case, that negative feedback might have been, "straighten the handlebars, you're leaning a little too far to the left," or "there's a curb over there, don't turn to the right."

He brought different CPGIs to his work at the EV rental startup.

With the board, his CPGI of choice was assurance. He shared revenue projections and market analyses and success stories. "We've got this," he essentially told them, "trust us, let us keep going."

With Sally, his CPGI of choice was pressure. He reminded her of her commitments, pushed her to hold up her portion of the company, and dangled the potential rewards of success in front of her. "We're so close," he promised her, "we can't stop now."

With the junior staffers and technical consultants, his CPGI of choice was structure. He set firm deadlines for specific, finite deliverables. He asked for regular reports. He provided an extremely clear set of expectations so that there could be no mystery about what is needed and when. "If you do your part and everyone else does theirs, just imagine what we'll accomplish together."

International ambitions

A few weeks after the mini-intervention, Eisen finalized his phase one map. In addition to the six American cities they had accounted for, he also included Toronto, Vienna, and Salzburg—three of the four cities that had previously felt like "reach" goals (London came with a few too many unique regulatory complications). He was *very* excited to show it off to the C-suite, to show them that they were poised to accomplish even *more* than their earlier objectives. That it was realistic. That an *international launch* was within reach.

Reception was mixed. It wasn't the slam dunk he expected.

"It's one thing to navigate different states at the same time, it's another to be answering questions about how to implement this in multiple *countries*," the director of product worried.

"We've always said how important it is for us to introduce EV rentals to cities in ways that are sensitive, intentional, and supportive of local communities. It's in our mission statement," the director of development reminded Eisen. "It's not that I think we *can't* scale to nine cities in three countries, it's that I don't think we can do that with integrity to our values."

Eisen bristled. To him, their values were a reason to spread access to EV rentals widely, as quickly as possible. The right regional reps would help them to execute on this—it wouldn't fall to the centralized team in Minneapolis to work out all the kinks about adapting to Austrian and Canadian markets. "We've set everything up already," he said, "we've opened the door. We can't get in our own way *now*."

But the meeting was clearly becoming a standoff. By now, Eisen had learned that sometimes the best thing to do was to give his team a chance to process. They usually came around after a few days.

That night, he stopped at the dojang for his twice-weekly taekwondo training, and came home in time to help his sons with their homework.

While throwing together mac and cheese, he spotted a few errors in Friedrich's homework, and pointed to it with the silicone spatula. "I before E," he recited, "like in your name. Use your eraser."

The silicone spatula: yet another CPGI.

The world needs you, Motivator, because...

- You lead with confidence, inspiring others to take action and believe in their own strength.

- You bring energy and passion, igniting enthusiasm and drive in those around you.

- You can sniff out systemic inequalities, corruption, and injustice better than anyone.

- You are innovators and trailblazers. You're willing to take risks and push boundaries. You live in the future, and are really good at building out scenarios.

- You embrace challenges, turning obstacles into opportunities for growth and success.

- You exude strength, showing how to face life's difficulties with courage and determination.

- You foster empowerment, encouraging others to step into their power and take ownership of their lives.

- You embody decisiveness, making bold choices that move things forward with clarity and purpose.

Mandatory attendance

Eisen received a text from the administrative coordinator the next morning. There was an emergency leadership team meeting at 10:00 a.m.

"I have a meeting with the UX team," Eisen texted back.

"This takes precedence," was the reply.

He knew that something was about to go down as soon as he entered the conference room. Sally's posture was too rigid and formal.

"I've realized that the best thing I can do for this team is to walk away," Sally declared. "You know I love you all, but we're at a turning point. You all need to turn one way, and I need to go another."

Eisen was stunned speechless. Sally had been one of his best friends since they were in the same cohort in business school. They had vacationed together. Helped each other through breakups and make-ups. They'd given toasts at each other's weddings. Eisen had no idea where Sally's decision was coming from.

The rest of the meeting was a rundown of the logistical next steps. A succession plan. A proposed one-month timeline to sunset Sally's responsibilities. A redistribution of company shares.

"But what is the other direction?" Eisen blurted out. "You said we need to turn one way and you need to go in another—what direction are you going in?"

Sally explained that her passion was and always had been strengthening her local community. It was the reason she was excited to create a vehicle rental service; to provide a sustainable and accessible mode of transportation that complemented Minneapolis's current public transportation infrastructures.

Now that the business was entering a stage of scaling and implementing, the focus seemed to be more on global trends, broad visibility, and a decentralized vision—all the things that Eisen had pointed to as priorities and the primary markers of progress. It wasn't that Sally disagreed with that vision, it just wasn't the scale she was motivated to work on.

"I need to focus on Minneapolis," Sally concluded. "That's always been my goal, to focus on my local community. I care about the rest of the world, but my heart is here."

Eisen bit his tongue. Any response he could come up with would have been death for his friendship with Sally.

So he nodded instead, said "thank you for letting us know," and retreated back to his office.

Sally's departure was going to be deeply disruptive, and she was quickly taking stock of everything that would need to be done in order to maintain the existing goals and timeline. There were meetings to schedule. Decisions to make. Provisions. Conversations. Recalculations.

For some reason, his face was feeling hot, and he could feel his pulse in his ears. But there wasn't time to deal with that. He needed to see if there was still time to catch at least a partial update from the UX team.

But before he could sit at his desk, he sent a text to Sally. "Will you help me chop firewood tonight?"

Eisen knew himself well enough to know that the best way to grease this particular wheel was to do something active with Sally. Over the years, these two friends had made habits of going on hikes, cleaning out their garages, tinkering with car engines, and, of course, chopping wood.

The first hour was mostly quiet. Methodical. Focused on placing, chopping, and piling.

But eventually the friends opened up to one another.

"You and me, we're gonna be okay," Sally assured him.

Eisen nodded.

"In fact, I think this'll be better for us to not have work constantly looming over our friendship."

Eisen brought the axe down again. *WHACK.*

"And that way I can stop holding you back."

Eisen put down the axe and looked at his friend. "Can you tell me why you're giving up now?"

Sally sighed and rolled her eyes. "*This* is why everyone quits on us, dude. You're always pushing us and telling us what we're supposed to do and how we're supposed to do it, and it's your way or the highway." She crossed her arms and sat down on the stump to face Eisen. "You've been pushing me in directions I don't agree we should go in, and then making me feel bad for not going there."

She recounted a few times when Eisen had pulled rank. It had been necessary for one of them to have a seat on the board and have a slightly "larger" vote on important matters, which was a power Eisen whipped out far more often than he wanted to—in theory.

"Maybe you're right and I'm wrong, but still..." Sally shrugged. "Do you know what it feels like? It feels like you have a cattle prod, and you're using it to make us do what *you* want us to do. Any time we stop to pause, or try to move in a different direction, or just do things in a way you don't understand, it's like *bzzt! Bzzt!* Here comes Eisen with the cattle prod, letting us know that we're in his way. So now, I feel like the best thing I can do is just get out of your way."

This sounded a whole lot like the attitude Eisen projected onto the junior staff who were constantly turning over, but it landed very differently coming from one of the co-creators of his vision. It absolutely gutted him to think that he might have made Sally feel bad.

That's because Eisen meant to *motivate* people with his CPGI, not discourage them or scare them away.

The CPGI

It's time for me to tell you what CPGI stands for: the Cattle Prod of Good Intentions. I can own this, because I'm a Motivator. The Cattle Prod of Good Intentions are the tools that Motivators use to encourage people on their journeys. They're the ways we help people to be productive, to move forward, to endure, and to stay on track.

We see CPGIs as the gentle encouragement of pool noodles Eisen used to support his son as he let go of his handlebars.

What we don't often realize is that there can be a shocker on the end of the CPGI. We don't see we can hurt people with our insistence that they keep going at the exact speed and in the exact direction that we know (okay, *believe*) is right, based on the data we have available to us.

Using pool noodles to keep Felix centered on the sidewalk is a totally reasonable and positive way of being a Motivator. But teaching your own child—who expressly wants you to teach them how to ride a bike, can only move in one direction, and obviously doesn't want to fall—is very different from collaborating with autonomous peers—who aren't always asking for your guidance, can move in several directions, are capable of choosing their own objectives, and take responsibility (and credit) for the outcomes.

Needless to say, people don't like to feel like cattle, even when Motivators prod them with the best of intentions.

Staffing update

Eisen needed to announce Sally's departure later that week. He was very used to delivering difficult news to the company in a focused and unemotional way. He'd done it enough times when announcing the departures of (sometimes multiple) junior staffers. But this was a big update, and the (true) rumor had clearly been circulating. Making a formal announcement would help make everything a lot less complicated and secretive.

But Eisen felt more implicated this time. Like he'd made an error. Like he'd missed something. Like the company was in jeopardy, and it was entirely his fault.

The feeling followed him around like a storm cloud. He moved through his meetings a little more distracted and detached than usual. Impatient to get the big announcement over with, but also dreading and avoiding thinking about it.

And when the day came, he stayed behind in his office for a moment, and pulled open one of his desk drawers. He took out a portrait of his family and reminded himself of a few things.

Try this: Cultivate Gravitas

Gravitas is when you feel safe, whole, and that you belong, and it can be cultivated.

In times of stress, we tell ourselves a story that we don't belong. But of course we belong. If we weren't meant to be here, we wouldn't be here.

In order to correct that story of not-belonging, you're going to remember a time when you felt a sense of belonging and try to recreate those feelings in your body.

Ugh, talking about feelings used to give me the willies. I *hated* talking about my feelings. Get that touchy-feely nonsense away from me![9]

A sense of belonging is one of the first things we need in order to experience gravitas.

First, think of when you feel you belong. Perhaps that's with your team at work. Maybe it's with your dogs or your friends.

Sit with a specific memory long enough that you can remember the details and sensations of it. If you can't remember the emotional feelings, try to remember the smells, tastes, textures, and sounds. What kind of weather do you associate with that memory? If you don't remember, make it up. Create a memory specific enough that you can reach back to it. Put it on speed-dial.

Then, try and return to that memory of belonging during low-stakes situations, like while you're bored waiting in line to get coffee, waiting for the warm water to kick in during your shower, or recovering between sets at the gym if you like

---

[9] We have a pillow with the "feelings wheel" in our house so that the kids can practice noticing and naming their feelings. I am not proud of this, but I was a jerk about my wife putting the feelings wheel in my face. I was so irritated about the stupid pillow. I was like, "Why did you buy *five* of them? They're in my face all the time!"

The thing is… there aren't five pillows, there's one, y'all. Just one. And it's just a pillow. And it is not in my face, it sits on the couch.

That's how icky talking about feelings used to make me.

going there. Can you invoke the feelings of belonging while going about your normal routine?

Next, try to return to that memory during increasingly higher stakes situations. Perhaps during a meeting with that client who stresses you out, while cleaning up a broken mug you're going to miss, or as the smoke detector is going off and won't. Stop. Beeping.

Finally, try and access the memory during moments where you feel a sense of *not belonging*. Maybe you are self-conscious at a gym where you feel like everyone is more affluent than you. Maybe you occasionally sit next to a relative who always belittles your political views. Maybe at a time when you, like Eisen, feel like you really messed up.

Keep calling back to that memory of belonging, and practice giving yourself a sense of gravitas. This will remind you that you belong wherever you are, and to focus on the positive aspects of the experience.

Go to book.vialucent.com to find more supporting material including a free, online course to cultivate more gravitas in your life.

Outro

Back on the running track.

Eisen believes in the people around him so much that he's pushing them all beyond their limits. This is super-duper dangerous. One person is going to sprint ahead, while someone else is going to stop and cry. The rope between them will go taut with pressure. It'll stretch out for a bit, and then *snap*! The rest of our bodies will be flung around, and we'll have an excruciating domino-effect demolition derby-style pileup. We'll all tumble spectacularly into the Petri Dish of Burnout.

But don't worry about him, he's about to make a different choice.

Let's leave him to it.

As a matter of fact, let's leave them all for a sec, and take a breather.

Take off the rope and come take a seat with me at the edge of the track. The others will keep running, while you and I have a chat. Don't worry, we're allowed to take a break. It's my metaphor; I make up the rules.

They can manage a lap without killing themselves... probably. Well, off they go.

Section 3

Cooldown

Lesson 8

Burnout has an opposite.

SUMMARY: The opposite of burnout is transformation, which is THE way of breaking any running-balls-out cycle. Transformation is different from change, in that you can transform WHAT you do, but you can only change HOW you try to do something. Transformation requires paying attention to your fear, which I describe as being like taking a peek at your body's poker hand. It's good, useful intel! I also review the stories from Lessons 4–7 and point out the ways in which each character's Awesome is also the energy source that turbocharges their method of running balls-out—Olive's inner critic, Trip's Wellness Mine, Fiona's Never-Ending Existential Research Project^{TM}, and Eisen's CPGI.

All right, dear reader. I left each of our characters on a cliffhanger on purpose. They're all on a precipice, where they are in a moment of choice. Perhaps you see that choice, like I do, but let's describe it and try to understand it.

They could choose to give up. (They won't).

They could choose to change the way they're doing what they're doing in order to keep going. Olive could hire a sales manager and find a new role for herself in the same company. Trip could find a way to hustle his butt off and carry his campaign over the finish line. Fiona could step far away from her job description and pitch an ambitious podcast strategy to a marketing team that didn't ask her to design one. Eisen could ghost his best friend and forge ahead with the people on his team who are willing to do anything he asks.

Or, they could transform what they are doing.

"Didn't you just say that?" you might be asking.

No, my dear, I said they could change, and that is very different from transformation. Think of it this way: if I change my socks, is that transformational? If I change my vocabulary, is that transformational? If I change my diet, is that transformati— actually, that'd be pretty transformational, bad example.

Okay, if I change from skim milk to 1%, is that transformational?

I know I'm being kind of sassy and splitting hairs here. What I'm getting at is that change is a scratch on the surface. Transformation cuts all the way down to the foundation. You can change how you do something, or you can transform what you're doing.

The biggest clue I can give you about the difference is that world scares the shit out of the mammal you're living in. Your body will tell you it is completely off limits—unless you are intentional about it.

Each of our characters was receiving that kind of feedback when we left them. The passion and energy that drove them into the righteous fight of doing meaningful work is now the same thing threatening to bring the whole team down into the Petri Dish.

The turning point

Now, you know what I'm all about, and you've noticed we're in the penultimate chapter of the book. You're probably very ready for me to turn our little tour bus away from the Debbie-Downer-bedtime-story marathon and towards the hopey-changey instruction manual.

We're so close. Stay with me in Debbie Downer land for another few moments.

We left off with Eisen, Fiona, Olive, and Trip *right* at the moment they were making a commitment to pursue a solution of **transformation**. This isn't dissimilar from where *I* was when I quit my job as an architect, hired David (my first coach), and created Via Lucent.

I want to point out what that kind of turning point *is* and what it *isn't*.

Let's start with what it isn't:

- It isn't a final answer.

- It isn't "I've figured it all out! Thank goodness I don't have to keep figuring it out anymore!"

- It isn't expertise or enlightenment or even a constant sense of certainty.

Sheesh, Laurie, you're rightfully wondering, what the heck is it?

- It is a commitment to the thing you are doing, sung in the key of an orgasmic "hell yes!"

- It is complete faith that you are working on the solution you have been dreaming of.

- It is both doing the work and training for the work that the world will call upon you to do in the future.

- It is being actively curious about how your thinking might expand or change in the future, and it is a willingness to appreciate when new insights reveal limitations in your previous ways of thinking—and an ability to accept that and move on.

After I made the choice to become a transformation guide, I started experiencing this recurring phenomenon (and I still do).

The best way I can describe it is that it's like I'm standing in a vast cathedral, exploring all of its intricacies. I look under the pews. Up in the Clerestory windows. Inside each sconce. And just when I think, *This is it, I've learned it all. I know it all,* I notice a little door in the corner. I go over, open it, and I become miniature-sized, like Alice in Wonderland. I go through and I'm not in a cathedral anymore. It's an athletic stadium that the cathedral was inside all along. On and on, I discover exponentially larger dimensions of understanding. A cavernous theater. A never-ending library. An enormous forest.

Olive, Trip, Fiona, and Eisen are letting go of their ambitions to sniff and re-sniff each and every sconce in one puny little cathedral—and learning how to do some interdimensional travel.

Transformation is scary when you're in it

For most people, really for anyone who has experienced trauma or vulnerability, doing this evokes a difficult emotional response. For goodness' sake, we're talking about stepping into a paradigm that is unfamiliar, counterintuitive, and emergent. In her book *Generation Dread*, Britt Wray brilliantly captures the wide range of emotional challenges that people face when they spend their lives focused on the immensity of climate challenges and the unknowability of climate solutions.

Dissonance. Betrayal. Overwhelm. Fear. Culpability. Impatience. Anger. Pity. Shock. And, of course, dread.

"A lot of distress is caused, not by difficult feelings themselves, but by the feelings we have about our difficult feelings. We judge ourselves negatively for feeling anything "negative," which paradoxically intensifies how terrible we feel"[10].

Let's focus on fear for a moment (although that is not the only emotion in play here). Fear's function in our existence is to let us know what to avoid. It tells us what *not* to think, do, or feel. Which people to avoid being around. Which sharp things to avoid puncturing our skin.

When fear speaks up, you get to say, "Oh, a new signal! There's a new signal I wasn't aware of."

If you listen with curiosity and do your best to learn and listen (and listen some more), to soften and find love for yourself, you can really learn from your fear. You can make use of this thing, which has caused you to avoid tasks or show up guarded, to lash out and snap, or to suppress your emotional needs.

In a way, when you study your fear, it's like getting a peek at your body's poker hand.

We've got to *look* at it. We've got to *notice* it. We've to *listen* to it. We've got to *see* where it shows up in our body. We've got to see what it *feels* like in our body. It is a supremely lucky thing when your subconscious mind shows you its cards—for goodness sake, *cheat*!

---

[10] Britt Wray, Generation Dread: Finding Purpose in an Age of Climate Crisis (Toronto: Knopf Canada, 2022), 129.

Change is the way to avoid fear, and thus let it control you.

Transformation is the way to confront your fear directly and blow its mind by becoming its student.

Transformation is the conscious, positive opposite of burnout. Both of them are turning points, but burnout is a crisis that happens *to* you, while transformation is a journey you *choose* to go on.

Now, the best case scenario of burnout is that it leads to transformation, but it's important to notice that they are not the same thing. When people run balls-out, they're usually trying to avoid burnout, but they're also unconsciously avoiding transformation. Our ragtag team has been skirting disaster for the last four chapters, but they're also fully capable of doing so. Transformation happens when each of us:

a) notices that we're running in a circle,

b) says, "Hey wait, this is fairly perilous and stupid,"

c) turns 90 degrees,

d) climbs out of the funnel, and

e) runs towards a better destination.

And that is my way-too-longwinded answer to the question, *is burnout necessary? Can we access our Awesome without it?*

After sitting with this question for over five years, I've arrived at a messy kind of response, which is that I think it's the wrong question.

I had wanted to know the answer, because if I knew it was possible to spare people from burnout, then all I'd need to do is help people hop over that step. In my well-meaning attempts to love people, I hoped to spare them the suffering. In my eagerness to improve the world, I wanted to help people access their Awesome as efficiently as possible. On the other hand, if it *wasn't* possible to spare people from burnout, I could at least help them optimize and expedite their visit to the Petri Dish. A quick skim over the "just visiting" corner of the "Go to Jail" square on the Monopoly board.

But burnout—and running balls-out—are ultimately only *symptoms*. They're the most dramatic and visible indicators that a person (or team) is facing an existential challenge. Those existential challenges can include external concerns like climate change, threat of societal collapse, systemic oppression, famine, and so on. But there are also existential *internal* challenges: a wounded look from someone you love, dismissal from a person you respect, fear of letting everybody down, that mean voice in your head telling you you're bad, useless, or broken. Those types of challenges threaten your sense of self and chip away at your conviction. In other words, they are challenges that hijack your Awesome.

Olive's Awesome is, among other things, the energy source of Evilo.

Trip's Awesome is, among other things, the open invitation to his Wellness Mine.

Fiona's Awesome is, among other things, the high quality of her next unfinished Never-Ending Existential Research Project™.

Eisen's Awesome is, among other things, the CPGI (the cattle prod of good intentions).

I've said before that your Awesome is both your greatest strength and a big clue about your worst habit. It's a sacred, tender aspect of your *self*. It's the thing that made it possible for you to accomplish all the amazing things you've done. It's the thing that has pulled at your heart and helped you find the courage to attempt brave, ambitious acts.

And, while it's done all of that, it's also probably what makes you different from other people. Your Awesome told you to take "the road less traveled by." I'm guessing that you stand by that choice, but it was still a sacrifice. Carving your own path was probably painful and costly. You probably had to leave old relationships behind. There are possibly still people who wish you were the person they thought you were. They're holding onto their memory of you as a predictable, safe person they understood. In some cases, they miss that person because they knew how to control them.

Honoring your Awesome is an active choice. For ambitious leaders, it's probably an obvious choice, and one that you might not even *realize* you made. But you made it, consciously or not. In fact, it's a *perpetual* choice. You make that choice every day, and you reinforce it every time you justify and defend it to people who prefer their made-up version of you.

If you're somebody who's ever "come out," you know exactly what I mean. Those of us who don't fit with (contextually) traditional, dominant, and normative scripts of gender, sexuality, or lifestyle have had a lot of practice making unpopular and often risky choices to resist expectation and interrupt assumptions in order to have integrity with ourselves.

And while you might not be *aware* that you've chosen to be true to your Awesome, you've never doubted it, either. It's never occurred to you to take the easy route. You can do anything you put your mind to—except that.

When a situation arises in which your Awesome is a weakness or a liability—as it did for Olive, Eisen, Fiona, and Trip—it's completely *terrifying*. It shakes the very core of the one thing in your life that has always felt unshakable, the thing you gave up safety for. When it becomes clear that you need to make a change, it's almost impossible *not* to internalize that as a signal that you are "wrong" or "bad." It introduces a nagging voice that tells you distracting lies. "The only possible reason you're failing is because everyone else sucks." "If you wanted this badly enough, you'd quit whining, stay up all night, and make it happen." "You must be a dumb-ass if the answers aren't already obvious." Worst of all: "If this isn't easy, it must mean there's something wrong with you."

Transformation is critically important, because we can't avoid the necessity of changing when *everyfuckingthing in the world is changing.* This has always been the case, but the rate of global change is accelerating. Now more than ever, the ways we already know how to be, how to do things, and how to *see* the world are not going to serve us in the world of tomorrow. Tomorrow won't be like yesterday.

Every single one of us is going to need to transform, but that necessity does not mean that we are flawed or broken. It just means that you can't know what tomorrow will call upon you to do yet, only that it won't be the same thing yesterday called upon you to do.

Duh.

Practice, practice, practice

So how do you prepare for an unknowable future? You identify how to contribute your Awesome to the current circumstances. You observe the world around you and the ways in which circumstances are changing. You make new choices about how to respond to those new circumstances and what they require from you and your Awesome. You develop the skill of doing that, repeatedly, over and over again, until you die. And you learn to not take it personally that you can't settle into a fixed, all-purpose approach.

In short: you practice the skill of **transformation**. You practice it as though your ability to help heal the world depends on it. Because it does.

All talented leaders—and the people who are wise enough to commit their talents to deserving initiatives—need to embrace opportunities for transformation throughout their lives if they have any chance of impacting the world of the future. Not just because leading involves maturing into our talents and stepping into our own power, but also because the world is transforming. If we want any kind of shot at responding to the amazing challenges and opportunities that our ever-changing world throws at our species, we're gonna have to change ourselves and the ways we work together to solve problems. That's the only way we'll be able to figure out how to thrive on this beautiful spinning rock for generations to come.

I've given you a couple suggestions of how to accelerate this work on your own: Balloon Breath, Body Alarm, Lover Words, and Gravitas. You might find other methods, but these are the easiest introductions to transformation and mindfulness. They're what made it possible for Olive, Trip, Fiona, and Eisen to resist falling into the Petri Dish of Burnout.

Speaking of, do you hear that?

They're coming back.

All right, let's get back in there. We're gonna do a cooldown lap with this crew. Now that you understand how distinct (yet similar) the ways each of the four types *could* wind up dragging us all down, we're going to see what happens when they choose to embrace transformation—and why *that* looks different for each person, too.

Lesson 9

Who you are is GOOD.

SUMMARY: I summarize the ways in which Olive, Trip, Fiona, and Eisen were able to achieve a sense of balance by wielding their Awesome more consciously. In other words: how they each transformed. I leave you with a pep talk about how we are headed into an unknown future, and that it is the boundless capacity of us humans that will give us everything we need in order to build that future.

The mood feels different somehow, lighter. We're running faster, but also more easily. Everyone's having more fun and feeling good.

Since you last saw them, our four teammates did things that might surprise you. Things that would seem out of character for how they used to think, feel, and act in the world. Let's catch you up to speed.

Olive

After resurfacing from a Balloon Breath, Olive opened her eyes and took in her computer screen. The first few applicants had already applied to the job listing she posted. *Briana Cox: Sales Representative Guru. Akash Chandrakar: Closer of Leads.* Remember, she had just gone down a deep self-deprecation spiral after a bad call with the Bezos Earth Fund, and had convinced herself that hiring a new sales rep would be better for the company.

When she allowed her mind to quiet, Olive noticed that the most grounded part of herself was whispering an important truth: there was a more authentic way that Olive could fundraise than the approach she had been taking for so long.

In her mind, new stories emerged. Stories that were kinder to her. Stories that accounted for her brilliance as a fundraiser. Stories that felt true, possible, likely, *inevitable*. There were so many better ways forward than agonizing over one grant.

So she rolled her eyes and quickly deleted the listing, not wanting to raise anyone's hopes for a job that didn't need filling.

Olive was a great fundraiser. Of *course* she was. She got to where she was by getting people excited. By bringing together groups of people. By finding common passions with perfect strangers.

When she remembered that, she realized that when she started working for the nonprofit, she began chasing the shiniest and biggest fundraising opportunities, simply because they were prestigious, not because they felt necessarily aligned. Set aside the international prizes that her nonprofit wasn't competitive for, and free up the easy-to-reach government grants. Forget about the Silicon Valley-based incubators, and focus on the local and mission-driven opportunities.

Olive does everything perfectly, but that's the kind of stuff she's best at because it keeps her going.

Perfectionists don't need to change, they just need help being strategic about where they commit their energy.

Some parting advice for Perfectionists:

- Embrace progress over perfection. It's okay if everything isn't flawless—your effort and dedication already make a world of difference.

- Celebrate small wins. Take a moment to appreciate the small victories; they're stepping stones to greater achievements.

- Be kind to yourself. Remember, your inner critic shouldn't run the show. Self-compassion is a much truer ally.

- Balance structure with flexibility. While routines ground you, a little spontaneity can bring unexpected joy and growth.

- Let others help. Collaboration doesn't diminish your strength—it enriches the process. Once you're working with other people, try to set realistic boundaries and ask for what you need.

- Practice relaxing, not perfecting. Rest is productive, too. Allow yourself to unwind without an agenda.

- Acknowledge your achievements. It's okay to take pride in your accomplishments; they're a testament to your hard work and dedication.

- Embrace imperfection in others, and eventually in yourself. People grow through encouragement, not criticism. Your empathy can be a guiding light.

- Loosen the reins sometimes. Trust that the world won't fall apart if things don't go exactly as planned. Practice flexibility and forgiveness, both for yourself and others. This is a way you can create stronger relationships and a more harmonious work environment.

- Focus on what brings you joy. Let passion, not just duty, guide you. Pursue what lights you up from within.

- You are worth more than your achievements alone. You are valuable simply for who you are, not just for what you do.

- Remember the bigger picture. Sometimes, stepping back to see the broader view can bring clarity and peace.

- Honor your emotions. Allow yourself to feel fully. Remember, your emotions are valid and a vital part of your experience.

Trip

A couple of hours after Trip's discreet scream in the stairwell, he returned to his office for a few easy tasks to give himself a gentle runway before his meeting with the campaign team. Remember, he received feedback that he was spreading himself too thin, and panicked when his personal trainer expressed a boundary around his herky-jerky schedule.

After checking his Body Alarm, Trip had noticed that his feelings of panic (which he envisioned as a tightness in his throat) could be reenvisioned as something for him to be curious about (a cartoonish frog who had taken up residence).

He took some time to notice, process, and become comfortable with it.

The campaign manager popped her head into the office to let him know the rest of the campaign team was in the conference room, ready to begin whenever Trip was. He picked up his new schedule and headed in.

As he walked in, he reminded himself that the most helpful thing he could do for his team was to be honest with them and ask for what he needed, rather than avoid acknowledging the moments when needs and expectations went unmet. Rather than let his boundaries dissolve into obsolescence as they were violated one by one. Rather than ignore the fact that their mistakes were consequential, just like their successes.

None of those things had actually created a safe working environment. In a way, it actually created a culture of disorientation and vigilance. No wonder Trip was envisioning tightness in his throat—things were being left unsaid. When the team's mistakes went unacknowledged, the team members themselves felt invisible. When their mistakes, like Vic showing up to volunteer training late and unprepared, were treated without importance, they felt that meant their *work* was unimportant, too.

Knowing that gave Trip a place to begin in his work of improving the culture at the campaign for everyone, beginning with himself.

He was very careful and delicate as he made a speech to his team about his need to pull back on his own involvement in their day-to-day work. His team found the whole thing to be a tiny bit overkill. Much ado about nothing. "Honestly, this all makes sense," said Vic, "I never expected you to show up to any of the volunteer trainings. I'm sorry that I wasn't ready in time for the one in June, but honestly, having you there made me a little nervous."

Others nodded. Trip asked if his presence had ever made them nervous, too. They wobbled their heads. "Kinda. Sometimes. Mostly when I don't expect you to be there."

Trip is heroic, especially because he is careful to notice when people need saving and when they simply need to be trusted.

Heroes don't need to change, they just need help knowing the difference.

Some parting advice for Heroes:

- Find ways to experience your own feelings, instead of defaulting to the feelings of those around you.

- You've been trained to obsess about how to achieve a goal. It's a hard habit to break because by midlife, you will default to doing what you've always known because it's comfortable. Instead, focus on how you want to *feel* when you achieve a goal. This is how you'll open up your ability to make things the world has never seen before.

- Embrace authenticity. It's okay to be vulnerable and let others see the real you. In fact, it fosters deeper connections than seeming "put-together."

- Celebrate rest as an accomplishment. Taking time to recharge is crucial. You don't have to be "on" all the time.

- It's okay to quit sometimes. You don't have to achieve everything.

- Prioritize meaning over recognition. Focus on the types of joy and fulfillment that can't be validated externally: self-care, quality time with loved ones, experiences in nature.

- Listen to your inner voice. Tune into your needs and desires; they're as important as your external goals.

- Balance doing with being. Life is about more than just accomplishments. Enjoy the present moment for what it is.

- Nurture your relationships. Invest time in your connections, even if they don't directly contribute to your goals. You can gain a lot by sharing your dreams with others.

- Find joy in the process. Achieving is great, but the journey can be just as rewarding if you let it be.

- Recognize the power of play. Engage in activities that are fun and purely for enjoyment, without an end goal.

- Try to dissolve your fears surrounding how you are seen. Many Heroes' worst fears are being seen as a failure, unprofessional, a double-dipper, or a non-expert. You can achieve balance by cultivating, experiencing, and expanding your emotions.

Fiona

By closing her computer at 10:00 p.m., Fiona had just pulled herself away from the brink of going down yet another rabbit hole. She made a decision *not* to die on the we-should-be-going-on-podcasts hill, and instead to step away from the marketing team meetings. Remember, she had just fought hard to clear up her schedule for things like this, which allowed her to use her thoroughness as a Researcher to help envision new opportunities for the company.

She had reviewed her Lover Words (which are private for her, so I won't tell you what they say), and reminded herself that this thing she wanted was not an appropriate use of her time and energy. That just because she *could* spend all night researching podcasts, make an impassioned appeal, and create an objective argument for her point-of-view doesn't mean that she *should*.

By having an intentional "lens" through which to look at this temptation, Fiona was able to respect and honor herself. Doing so would make it possible for her to show up fully in the capacities that were more worthy of her.

It took a few weeks for the transition to settle, but in the grand scheme, this was time well spent.

Fiona crafted the right schedule for herself, and even slightly adjusted her job description. Now that Fiona felt worthy of being in the meetings she was in, she began having new thoughts, which allowed her to make new choices. She became able to say things with a different tone of voice that exuded more confidence. She became able to listen better, to synthesize ideas better.

You get different outcomes when you feel worthy of being where you are, that you belong, that you are safe.

Now, you might think that once you get a high-achiever like Fiona in a new work situation that is actually a good container for her energy, that's where all her energy would go. That she wouldn't need or want another outlet for her Awesome, because she found the right one, like the heroine in a rom-com who, after the credits, is definitely going to abandon the friends who were there all along.

Not so. She actually recommitted herself to an artistic passion in addition to her job.

When I first met her, Fiona was squirreling away spare hours on Tuesday nights because it was the only leisure time she had available. She was settling for the only dance class being offered in town at that time, but that wasn't gonna scratch her itch— it was a consolation prize, a pacifier. The mere dregs of a hobby. When you settle for "what you can get," all you're left with is an hour or two to go through the motions. Literally, in Fiona's case.

Fiona didn't run out of energy for dance because she had finally landed in a work environment that she could pour herself into. Quite the opposite; she received enough energy from her work that she was able to invest more in her creative pursuits, which energized her differently in turn.

Instead of hiding parts of herself from one another, she showed up wholly at work, home, and in her art. In a balanced life, this creates abundance.

We're so used to a scarcity mindset, believing that when we give all of ourselves to one aspect of our lives, it runs out. We create capitalist metaphors for things like attention (which we "pay"), time (which we "spend"), and even love (which can look like "cashing in" on favors). But unlike money, which runs out, our life spirit is limitless, with the ability to blossom continuously, getting wider and larger with every act of love.

Fiona is a prolific and effective researcher because she is careful to investigate the things that require her close attention, *including her own need for emotional expression.*

Researchers don't need to change, they just need help turning the magnifying glasses towards their own hearts.

Some parting advice for Researchers:

- Step out of your mind. It's safe to engage with the world outside your thoughts; it's full of enriching experiences.

- Challenge your tendency to stay in the background. You make world-class observations, and we won't know what they are if you don't tell us.

- When you're challenging conventional wisdom, you'll probably find that your feelings get out of balance and you react emotionally. When that happens, get curious about this and ask yourself, "Which part of myself am I dishonoring when I do this?" You can make even more valuable contributions if you learn to access and integrate your feelings more fully.

- Seek connection. Relationships can provide just as much nourishment as knowledge. Invest in them.

- Trust your instincts. You don't have to know everything before you take action; sometimes, intuition is a usable type of wisdom.

- Allow yourself to be seen. You have so much to offer—don't hide behind the comfort of solitude.

- Celebrate collaboration. Working with others can enhance your ideas and bring new perspectives.

- Recognize your impact. Your thoughtful presence makes a difference. Trust that your contributions matter.

Eisen

Eisen looked at his family portrait, and remembered the sensations from a picnic they shared together when the boys were much younger. His life felt so whole that day, he felt such a sense of coherence and belonging, basking in the warmth of a perfect sunbeam. He remembered the mild, clean aroma of baby powder, and the acidic tang of the cured meats and cheeses he and his wife had selected to picnic on. The welcome soundtrack of a busking guitarist playing groovier versions of his favorite oldies.

Remember, Eisen was looking at a photograph of this scene in the minutes before announcing to his company that his best friend and co-founder had chosen to resign, for mostly interpersonal reasons.

Doing this reminded Eisen that he was capable of both accepting Sally's departure in the company and trusting in his own goodness. That giving people opportunities to make their own choices was a respect he owed them. That the resistance he noticed in his team was a thing to be curious about, not necessarily a thing to prod out of sight—even with a supportive pool noodle.

And it was with that clarity that Eisen was able to really *hear* what Sally had been saying. He rushed to the conference room, spotted her, and grabbed her for a quick sidebar in the lobby.

"I totally get why you don't want to be with us while we focus on branching out," Eisen said, "but you know what we're doing and you care so much about it, and I'd hate to lose those things. Would you think about being our rep? For Minneapolis?"

This took Sally by surprise. It hadn't occurred to her, but it was an intriguing next step. Technically it was a step *down*, but one that might really suit her. She'd have to talk it over with her wife, but she said, "You know what, I'd like to think about it."

Whatever she decided, Sally had felt seen. And Eisen had seen more.

Eisen is a Motivator who is capable of being sincere, helpful, and authentic... especially because he is able to ground himself and operate from a place of attunement. Motivators don't need to change, they just need help framing their choices of what to support in other people, and how.

Some parting advice for Motivators:

- Balance strength with vulnerability. It's okay to show your softer side; it deepens your connections with others.

- Exploring your emotions and how others are feeling will bring you balance. Can you find safe ways to practice that?

- Practice patience. Not everything requires immediate action. Sometimes, waiting can lead to better outcomes. Other times, your job is to accept that you can't force your way through every challenge.

However, you *can* build your capacity to make better and new choices.

- Lead with empathy. Your power is magnified when paired with understanding and compassion.

- Allow for rest. Your energy is a gift, but even the strongest need to recharge. Take time to pause, reflect, and restore.

- Recognize the power of softness. Strength isn't just about force—it's also about gentleness and care.

- Seek balance in control. You don't have to manage everything alone. Allow others to share in the responsibility.

- Honor your journey. Your passion and drive are forces for good. Embrace the path you're on, knowing you are making a profound impact.

Escape from the funnel

All right everyone, let's quit circling the Petri Dish and make our way out of here by turning 90°—that's 90°to the *right*, to be sure—and get out of here.

Over the top of the funnel we go, and the path is downhill from here.

You, me, Olive, Trip, Fiona, and Eisen, we're keeping a steady pace—but being careful not to let inertia embarrass us.

We're nearing the end of our run, and I think you're going to like where we end up.

When I'm getting deep in conversation with highly ambitious leaders (which is a thing I do at pretty much any opportunity), we usually touch on the subject of our own early childhoods. What I've found is that we tend to have a shared experience of having been children who exhausted the adults around us by asking too many existential questions.

"Mommy, what is a watch? How does it work? What is *time*?"

"Ms. Patterson, how do we know that the scientific process leads to objective knowledge?"

"Uncle Jin, how big is the universe? What shape is it?"

That last question comes up a surprising amount. People who want to change the universe want to have a solid concept of the thing they're trying to change, which requires having a mental model.

Not being the child of astrophysicists, I had to look up the answer myself.

One way of defining "the universe" is with the concept of the heliosphere. You might remember that "helio" refers to the sun; the "heliosphere" is "the region surrounding the Sun and the solar system that is filled with the solar magnetic field and the protons and electrons of the solar wind."[11]

In other words, it is the massive chunk of space on which the sun exerts its influence. Beyond the heliosphere, it's as though the sun doesn't exist. In some ways, the heliosphere is existence itself, represented as a finite physical space.

Let that sink in for a moment.

Did that blow your mind? Well, get ready, because I'm gonna do it again when I tell you this next thing.

You and me, baby, the place where we're headed... it's *beyond the heliosphere*. We're going to a place where we don't exist yet. We're not consuming reality anymore, we're creating reality. Beyond the heliospheric barrier, it's like we're operating backstage, writing the script and setting the scene for a play that hasn't opened yet.

As I write this in 2025, I'm watching as the terrifyingly unknowable force of AI accelerates every other technology, without any kinds of guardrails. I'm watching meteorological reporting where record-breaking weather events have begun to feel ubiquitous. I'm watching as global superpowers make

---

[11] Brittanica.com/science/heliosphere

sharp right turns in lockstep like synchronized swimmers. I'm watching as new generations step into the power of self-knowledge, integrity, and authenticity at younger and younger ages.

Progress and destruction are both happening at exponentially faster speeds. Everything is expanding. Everything is falling apart.

In order to come into your full Awesomeness, you need to do things you've never done before. I hope this book has demonstrated to you that *you will burn out if you keep trying to maintain your Awesome in the same way that you currently know how to.* This is true whether you're a startup founder hoping to go global, a governor running for federal office, or a student preparing for graduation.

And you're gonna be brilliant at this because:

1. you have a powerful energy source within you,

2. in fact, you basically *are* a powerful energy source,

3. and you already *know* that you have that frickin' powerful energy.

All downhill from here

Now that you've read this book, you have a few reminders of how to avoid running balls-out and, instead, go out into society and be that energy source.

As I've mentioned before, I work primarily with people who work in climate. But I know a few things about renewable energy that people in the climate fields rarely talk about.

There's a popular misconception that ideas and technologies are, by themselves, the solutions to our problems. Solar panels, wind turbines, carbon capture, heat pumps, electric vehicles, regenerative agriculture, sustainable design, and so on.

But the truth is that *people* are the solutions, not the ideas and technologies they produce.

The only thing that will heal the world is for people to have access to the best data and wisdom.

And for them to use those data and wisdom as they transform themselves and the world around them.

The real solution to our climate woes is for people like you to go out into the world with all of your Awesome.

And to activate everyone else's Awesome.

It's the only solution.

That's renewable energy, baby.

Let's stop here, on the shore of this lazy river.

And let's jump in.

Heck, I'm already naked. Eisen's jumped in ahead of me, and Trip's helping Olive find the courage. Fiona will make her way in eventually.

You look hesitant. You're afraid the water will feel cold. You're making excuses not to go in.

I understand. I see you.

But I also see how, when you do stupid things like run balls-out, you're bringing yourself closer and closer to a vacation in the emergency room. The heartbreaking thing is that you do it for *us,* because your wild activist heart won't let you stop.

I see how you give and give and give. I see how you stretch yourself out of alignment with who you are for the sake of progress and action. I see how you sacrifice something within yourself in the name of progress.

I see that you won't draw finish lines.

I've been there.

I learned at such a young age to suppress my body's fear response that by the time I was baffled about going to the ER for my stroke, I was no longer in touch with any of my body's survival instincts. I was drained, and my body decided that it was sick of trying to warn me.

Your body can make you take a vacation in the ER. None of the paths in this part of the landscape end well.

I see how you suppress your survival instincts in the name of ambition. I spent 238,784 hours in that mode between the ages of four and 45. Between backing down from my first attempt to shed a name that felt uncomfortable for me, and having a gender-affirming top surgery that wound up as front-page news, that is 14.3 million minutes. I help people move quickly through this change because the behaviors you think are hidden are glaringly obvious to me.

This is the time to unpeel the ways you cope with the false message that who you are is not "good."

In early 2022, my coach said to me, "You get to decide how you want to feel. And you have such a right to decide this, that you can make it a sovereign declaration in your life." Sound familiar? This is when I chose my Lover Words from lesson 6.

She asked me, "How do you want to feel?"

I thought, and I thought, and I worked on my words, distilling an endless stream of rumination into just three words. I didn't know any transgender people who felt *safe*, *whole,* and *belonging*. And I thought, that sounds right. *That's* what I want to do. I want to feel safe and whole, and I want to belong everywhere I choose to go. It was as easy as deciding to do it with conviction. I adopted this as a sovereign declaration and I used it as a filter to decide what in the world was for me and what was not for me. And I had already done this lift by the time I decided to get surgery and live finally in the body that I wanted to live in.

Our friends are all in the water now. Olive, Trip, Fiona, Eisen. Bathing, meditating, relaxing, exploring. They were resistant to transforming their lives at the same time they were consciously trying to do so. They felt exhausted and futile, and they didn't know how to move forward.

So I'll tell you what I told them: you don't have to keep living like that. I mean it literally, and I understand how hard that might be for you to believe right now.

But I know, and you will come to know this as well, that in our cores, we are totally unlimited. I know we can be safe and whole. We belong everywhere we choose to go. Even this freezing cold river.

This might feel like a dark and scary path for you, but I've been down it so many times that I would do it barefoot at night in a rainstorm, holding a sleeping baby and an armful of kittens. It never occurs to me anymore that I'm not safe. It feels good to be able to notice when I'm in a survival emotion, and it feels good to know how to get back into creation whenever I want. There is nothing scary left on this path for me.

It feels so good to be at home in the skin you live in. It feels so good to belong everywhere you go without question. If I could bottle this and give it to everyone on the planet, I would. Because you are capable of so much more than you realize—once you learn to treat your fear as your teacher.

Jump into the river, chilly and life-giving.

I'm not going to let anything bad happen to you. Promise.

Prologue

Who you are is GOOD.

This sentence is on the back of my business cards, on my website, on the packages I send to clients, and I have a pile of stickers I hand out too.

It is what the end of the journey of working with me feels like: That your innate self is GOOD and that you belong. Here's the long version I'll say to you if we get the chance to meet:

(Name), the you who is you at the core, the you who has always been there and will always be there, the one you know through and through, is uniquely, beautifully, divinely GOOD and we need you.

I wrote this book as a love letter to my past, present, and future clients. I wrote it in a way that you all could get something out of it and feel better. I wanted it to be of value to you on its own.

If you've gotten this far and are yearning for more, why not enroll in one of my courses or work with me one on one?

If you can decide that you are worthy of feeling better, getting the results you've dreamed of, improving your relationships with your inner circle humans, and enjoying life more, then hire me. My promise to you is that, if you do, I'll guide you through transformation that will impact every corner of your life you let it into.

What are you waiting for?

You can find me at vialucent.com or on LinkedIn. I really do accept all connections and answer messages.

You can find more resources about the book at book.vialucent.com.

About the Author

Laurie McGinley is super f'n magic. She guides World Changers through the barriers that prevent you from making your dreams reality.

She takes the approach that it's not her job to tell you how to do yours, she's here to wake you up about what you can't see, teach you how to see it, and upgrade how you show up for your work so that you can get out of your own way.

McGinley has a deep meditation practice that has transformed every corner of her life. If you ask her about it at a party, you should go get a snack because you'll be there for a while.

Her family motivates her to find new ways to do better every single day and is grateful for their presence in her life.

When not guiding World Changers through transformation and being with her family, she is a wood turner and carver who absolutely will pull over in traffic to put a good-looking log in the back of the car.

McGinley lives in Saint Paul, Minnesota, USA on Dakota land.

www.ingramcontent.com/pod-product-compliance
Lightning Source LLC
Chambersburg PA
CBHW020408150626
46554CB00012B/413